An Executive's Guide:

Incentive and Nonqualified
Stock Options

An Executive's Guide:

Incentive and Nonqualified
Stock Options

Peter R. Wheeler

CLU, ChFC, CFP, CIMC

Family Office Publishing
For information, contact:
Allyson Phillips
2665 Fourth Avenue
San Diego, CA 92103
619-491-0225
alw@wheelerfrost.com

Cover design by Shandley Phillips

International Standard Book Number 0-9714898-0-7

Printed by Carter Press of San Diego

To my family and my associates who provided the support to complete this project.

Table of Contents

Foreword

A few years ago our firm was approached by a new client who had a substantial number of stock options issued by his company. He needed our guidance on how and when to exercise his options. He planned on selling some stock after exercising his options in order to diversify his portfolio and then give us the money to invest. While his situation was a bit more complex than most, it was not unique and we did not anticipate any great problems with his request.

As I set out to learn about the various issues affecting our client and to develop a plan to mitigate the tax consequences and other issues surrounding his situation, I was amazed to find that there was very little information available for executives or their advisors regarding stock options. I also found that there was no effective tool to analyze the effects of exercising options. The questions to answer were numerous:

Which options do I exercise?
When do I exercise them?
Do I hold them once I exercise?
When should I sell?
What are the tax consequences of my decisions?

At the time we had to design our own spread sheet to handle these questions. Since then, several commercial products have become available to help professionals and executives analyze their stock option choices. These programs vary in their usefulness, however, all require that the user has some prior knowledge of stock options.

The first edition of this book was published in December, 2000. At that time we were just beginning to see the impact of the dot com collapse. Since then it seems, we have had to deal more with what to do with "underwater" options and lost fortunes than with tax planning for gains on exercised options. In fact, interest in stock options has substantially waned. Many employers now report that prospective employees don't even want stock options as part of their benefit package.

Millions of unexercised options remain and even those that are now underwater may return to value. As the stock market improves, there will be renewed interest in options as a valuable part of an overall benefit package. As the Enron debacle forces changes both to the laws governing the granting and taxation of stock options and to the way companies use stock options as employee incentive compensation, we may well see the stock option regain its rightful place, encouraging ownership and employee interest.

Introduction

The Importance of Stock Options

Stock options are not new. For years they have been used as a perk for senior management. What is new, however, is the extent to which stock options are now a major part of the compensation package and wealth of the average worker. A recent study by The Federal Reserve Board found that 37% of companies offering stock options have broadened them to include many nonexempt employees. Another study by Oppenheimer Funds in 1999 found that 10% of private sector employees held stock options. That would be about 12 million American workers. The National Center for Employee Stock Ownership in Oakland, California, estimates that 10 million non-management employees held nonqualified stock options (NQSOs) at the end of 2000. This compares to just one million at the end of 1992. A tenfold increase in just eight years! The National Center's study found that 74% of the responding companies granted options to non-management employees. Oppenheimer estimates that 50% of all public companies offer stock options to all employees. A more recent study by Option Wealth, Inc., of Rockville, MD, puts option ownership at 14.1 million workers holding $522 billion of option value. Since then, of course, we have had the collapse of the dot coms and the bear market of 2000/2001.

The Oppenheimer study also found that employees viewed stock options as a major factor in deciding to accept a job. However, many said they knew more about *Einstein's Theory of Relativity* than they did about the taxation of their stock options. The study painted a graphic picture of just how little is known about stock options by the employees who hope to benefit from them.

> *"Many people today probably take more time reading the nutritional information on a jar of spaghetti sauce than they take reading their option agreements."*
> Marci Rossell, Chief Economist, Oppenheimer Funds

The Oppenheimer study also found that:

> 74% said they know very little about their stock options.
> 52% didn't know the tax consequences of exercising their options.
> 50% think their company's stock will do better than the market.
> 34% didn't know if they had ISOs or NQSOs.
> 75% didn't know about the Alternative Minimum Tax (AMT).
> 11% had let their options expire "in-the- money."

When Oppenheimer asked the respondents what kind of options they had, no one was able to respond. However, when asked if they had incentive stock options or nonqualified stock options, 30% were able to respond.

Stock options have generated tremendous wealth. According to iQuantic, a San Francisco consulting firm, options generated more than $500 billion of wealth in 1999 alone. However, iQuantic's annual study of technology companies found that the median value of a stock option grant was only $20,000 to $30,000. While more than 160,000 high-tech company employees became millionaires in 1999; clearly, many option holders will not become overnight millionaires. Even the smallest option holder will face many of the same questions about tax consequences and option exercise strategies that CEOs have faced for years.

Average Value of Grant by Job Category	
	Value of Grant
Executives	$511,804
Senior Managers	139,375
Middle Managers	57,208
Salaried Technical	35,481
Salaried Nontechnical	22,708
Sales	51,762
Hourly	7,982

Unfortunately, this sudden explosion of stock option holders has caught the advisory community by surprise. Many accountants, attorneys, financial planners, and stock brokers know little more about stock options than their clients. Additionally, there has been very little in print that either advisors or option holders could turn to for guidance. While the void is beginning to fill, much of the information is too technical for the lay person.

Many of the questions I had to find answers to as I started to work with our stock option clients are answered in this book. I have made every attempt to keep the answers understandable. This is a very complex area of the law and I don't want you to be among the 52% who don't know the tax consequences of your options. However, I don't anticipate that this book will make you an expert either. Because state laws vary greatly, this book does not address them. Use this book as a guide to help in your understanding of this very valuable asset that your employer has provided you. Make sure that you have a qualified advisor working with you to insure that you maximize the value of your assets.

Since these studies were completed, we have seen the demise of most of the dot com companies, the collapse of Enron and Global Crossing and substantial stock price drops in industry giants such as Lucent Technologies, Cisco Systems, and Qualcomm. Even non-technology stalwarts such as Home Depot and Wal-Mart lost market value during the 2000/2001 bear market. As a result, for the moment, stock options have lost some of their charm. But, while market value may have been lost and many stock options are underwater, the options remain. In many cases, the option holder will eventually reap a profit.

> *"An average of 19% of 401K plan assets were in company stock at the end of 2000."*
> Investment Company Institute

Hopefully, we have learned a lesson from this. As noted in the Oppenheimer Study, most employees, in the late 1990s, believed that their company's stock would grow faster than the market as a whole. Through the late 1990s that may have been the case. But, in just two short years much of that excess growth had been eliminated, leaving many stock option holders devastated, and many financial advisors feeling that they had preached the need for diversification to a disinterested congregation. Between their 401K plans, pension plans, and stock options, employees from the boardroom to the mail room had 60 to 80% of their worth tied up in the same company that they depended on for their income, health insurance, and long-term security. When the company collapsed, all was lost. Maybe now, before the next big sell-off, employees will take to heart the **Core Capital**ᵗᵐ concept discussed later in this book.

Percent of 401K Plan Held in Company Stock

Company	Percent
Proctor & Gamble	95
Pfizer	86
Coca Cola	82
GE	77
Texas Instruments	76
McDonalds	74
Enron	62
Ford	57
Quest	53
AOL/Time Warner	52

Chapter One

What Are Stock Options?

What is a Stock Option?

Generally, a stock option is a right granted to the holder of the option to be able to purchase a certain number of shares of a stock at a stated price within a given time period. There is no requirement to exercise the option even if the stated price is reached.

There are two main types of stock options: exchange traded stock options and employer grant options. **Exchange traded stock options** are stock options that trade on the various stock exchanges and may be bought and sold in much the same fashion that the stocks themselves are. **Employer grant options** are rights granted by employers to employees as part of compensation packages. All options have a **strike price**, an **expiry date**, and a stated number of shares to which the option applies.

> The **strike price** is the price at which the option can be exercised or purchased, regardless of its market price.

What are Exchange Traded Options?

Exchange traded stock options are sold (written) by investors who hope to make money on the swings in the stock's price. A **call option** grants the holder (buyer) the right to buy the stock away from the seller (writer) of the call. A **put option** grants the buyer the right to sell the stock at the strike price. Both are at a stated price (strike price) above or below the price of the stock on the date the option is written and are exercisable on or before a specific date. A **covered option** means the writer of the option owns the stock. A **naked option** means that the writer of the option does not currently own the stock upon which the option is written. Once written, these options are often traded and take on a value of their own depending on the market price of the stock versus the option strike price and the time remaining to the option's expiry date. **See Chapter Thirteen.**

What are Employer Grant Options?

Employer grant options were once reserved for the narrow ranks of senior executives. Today, many firms include middle management and other employees in their stock option plans. As a result, many employees have found themselves with millions of dollars of potential wealth tied up in their employer's stock option plan.

Employer grant options are intended to provide employees with a vested interest in making the company profitable. To the extent that the company's successes are reflected in the growth of the company's stock price, then the employee will share in the gains through stock options. Employer grant options are restricted and are only available to the company's employees, members of the board, and consultants.

Generally, all employer grants are referred to as **compensatory stock options** because they are a part of the company's compensation plan. They are also known as **incentive stock options** because of their incentive-based purpose. There are actually four types of employer grant stock options: **stock appreciation rights, phantom stock, incentive stock options, and nonqualified stock options**.

What are Stock Appreciation Rights and Phantom Stock?

Stock appreciation rights (SARs) and **phantom stock** are really pseudo-options. While employee incentives, they are not actually stock options. These pseudo-options do not actually offer ownership in the company. Rather, they offer a conditional bonus based on the future performance of the company. Most often these plans are offered by non-public companies where the value of the company's stock is not determined by open market trading. **See Example 1.1.**

The variations of SARs are unlimited. There are no tax benefits to such plans and no statutory requirements. For the benefit of the employer and participating employees, they should be carefully thought out and presented in writing. I would strongly recommend that a qualified attorney draft the document. This book does not address SARs and phantom stock options.

What are Nonqualified Stock Options?

Nonqualified stock option (NQSO) plans are the most popular plans. In spite of the less desirable tax consequences, they offer substantially greater flexibility than incentive stock options, thus increasing their popularity. There is no limit on the dollar amount or number of shares that may be granted to an employee. NQSO grants may be made to owners of more than 10% of the stock who are employees, board members, or consultants. Taxation at exercise is the same as on your regular compensation as an employee. **See Chapter Three.**

Example 1.1 Jones Company, Inc., a closely held corporation, has only one shareholder, Mr. Jones. Mr. Jones doesn't want to share ownership with his employees, but does want them to take a vested interest in growing his business. Mr. Jones develops a formula to fairly determine the current value of the business. He then develops a SAR that provides that his three key managers will share in the growth of the business above that point based upon some triggering event, such as his retirement.

What is an Incentive Stock Option?

Incentive stock options (ISO) are also known as **statutory stock options** because they are subject to a strict set of statutory regulations. As a result, they also offer significantly better tax benefits than nonqualified stock options. Since all options are granted to create an incentive, they are often all referred to as incentive stock options. It is important to determine which type of option is actually involved because the benefits and restrictions will differ. **See Chapter Four.**

What is an Employee Stock Purchase Plan?

Employee Stock Purchase Plans (ESPP) are also statutory stock plans and are subject to a strict set of statutory regulations. They are often referred to as "Section 423 plans" as they are governed by IRC Section 423. Under an ESPP employees use after-tax payroll deductions to purchase company stock at a discount of usually 15%. Surveys have shown that 75% or more of the companies offering ESPPs offer Section 423 plans. However, about 25% offer a nonqualified ESPP. These plans are known as "open market purchase plans" and do not offer the tax benefits of a Section 423 plan. It is important to know which plan you have. **See Chapter Five.**

A Comparison of ISOs and NQSOs

Feature	ISOs	NQSOs
Tax - date of grant	No tax impact	No tax impact
Tax - date of exercise	FMV - EC = Preference item for AMT on Form 6251	FMV - EC = Ordinary Income on Form 1040
Tax - date of sale if held for one year	FMV - basis = Capital Gain (basis = EC + offset for AMT if applies)	FMV - basis = Capital Gain (basis = EC + Ordinary Income at execution)
# options issued	$ limit	Unlimited
$ limit on options issued	$100,000	None
Alternative Min. Tax	Subject to	Not subject to
Ordinary income tax	No	Yes
Withholding, FICA, Med.	No*	Yes
Capital Gains	Yes	Yes
Deductible to Corporation	No	Yes
Transferable	No	Yes

FMV = Fair market value

EC = Exercise cost

AMT = Alternative Minimum Tax

*IRS Notice 2001-14 requires FICA taxes to be withheld for options exercised after Dec 31, 2002

Chapter Two

Why Do Companies Offer Stock Options?

Why do companies offer stock options?

Prior to the 2000/2001 Bear market, it was estimated that nearly 10% of all public sector employees held stock options. In the technology sector, more than 50% of all companies issued stock options. For new companies such as the pre-IPO Internet or new technology start-ups, granting stock options was essential in order to attract the talent necessary to build the company's franchise. Employers must have something different from others in order to attract the best talent. For many potential employees this is the opportunity to hit the jackpot on appreciated company stock. Additionally, there is the motivation and teamwork that can come from employees, even at the lowest levels, knowing that they will directly benefit from the company's success as a result of their collective hard work.

Only time will tell just how much has been impacted by the 2000/2001 Bear market. However, we know that many prospective employees now are much more interested in job security than they are in stock options. The fierce competition for talent has also waned with the dot com demise. Software companies are paying a fraction of what they paid for qualified software engineers a few years ago and have an abundance of applicants. However, millions of unexercised options remain. As the market improves and the economy recovers, it is hard to imagine that stock options will not regain a prominent role in new benefit packages.

Are there tax benefits for the corporation?

Under current tax laws, NQSOs are tax deductible compensation on the company's tax return at the time they are exercised by the employee. The employee must recognize the NQSOs as income at the time of exercise so it is logical that the company can take a corresponding deduction. However, since there is no actual cost to the company, there is no reduction to the company's earnings. No tax is associated with the exercise of an ISO, so there is no benefit to the corporation for the exercise of an ISO. **See Chapter Six.**

Are stock options chargeable to corporate earnings?

No. Neither the option grant nor the exercise is chargeable to the company's earnings. This is part of the attraction to the company. It costs nothing to grant the option.

A little history on this is enlightening. In the 1950s, the American accounting rules-making body, the Accounting Principals Board (APB), now known as the Financial Accounting Standards Board (FASB), commissioned a study on how to determine the value of an option. The commission could not agree on a value so the APB decided the value was zero with no charge to earnings.

In 1993, the FASB, with the encouragement of Congress, proposed regulations requiring a charge to earnings. The American Electronics Association responded with a study claiming that a charge to earnings for stock options would cause the typical Silicon Valley firm's profits to decline by 35%. That would cause options not to be granted to lower employees. FASB made no change to the old APB position.

Since 1993, stock option grants have exploded. For example, General Electric's CEO, Jack Welch's options soared from $4.4 million to $29.9 million. In December 1997, Michael Eisner, Walt Disney's CEO, exercised $570 million worth of options in a single day. This may be changing, however. The British Accounting Standards Board has proposed that U.K. companies charge the estimated present value of stock options against earnings. Additionally, the Enron debacle has brought Congressional attention to the impact stock options played in the company's demise. This could reopen the debate in the United States.

Are there any rules of thumb for how many options a company should grant?

The variety of stock option plans equals the number of companies issuing them. However, Salary.com suggests that a good rule of thumb is that each tier in the organization should get half the options granted to the tier above. **See Table 2.1.**

Table 2.1

Position	shares
CEO	64,000
Senior VP	32,000
VP	16,000
Asst. VP	8,000
Manager	4,000
Senior Tech.	2,000
Entry-level	1,000

Is stock option accounting distorting company profits and the economy?

Bernstein Research believes that stock options and the dubious accounting behind them are distorting the stock market, corporate balance sheets, and the overall economy. According to Bernstein's Michael L. Goldstein, in early 2000, the intrinsic value of outstanding options at the end of 1999 was half a trillion dollars, equal to 35% of corporate debt.

Option grants were up a whopping 57% in 1999, $101 billion, which came to 13% of corporate earnings. Corporations do not take these options as an expense. Over the three years ending in 1999, had the 45% annual growth in option awards been expensed, earnings growth would have been 5.3% a year, not 8.7%. This added 8% to 10% annual earnings growth over the period to high-tech stocks which represented half the growth rate of that sector. "The in-the-money value of unexercised options outstanding now equates to 22% of the book value of equities," Goldstein says, ". . . and in technology, the share is over 80%."

If options were treated as a liability, the debt-to-equity ratio of high-techs would zoom from 16% to 99%. The benefits of the options have already been realized on the bottom line, but the $500 billion bill for the options has not been paid. Companies that give out options take one of three courses:

They can expense them, something most won't do.

They can run the printing press and crank out more shares.

They can choose not to expense the options and then buy stock back to hold down dilution.

The bottom line is that while options are great for the employee, they definitely have a distorting effect on the company's bottom line and the economy.

How insightful Mr. Goldstein was. Two years later the dot coms had collapsed and the technology sector was severely down. They took with them much and, in some cases, all of the in-the-money value that Mr. Goldstein spoke of. Robert J. Samuelson of *Newsweek,* in a February, 2002 article for the *Wall Street Journal*, The Use and Abuse of Stock Options, used Enron's failure to encourage his readers ". . . to search for deeper causes, beginning with stock options." Mr. Samuelson said that "Stock options foster a corrosive climate that tempts many executives, and not just those at Enron, to play fast and loose when reporting profits." In 2000, the typical CEO of the top 350 companies earned $2.5 million with half of that coming from stock options according to William Mercer, Inc.. For Cisco Systems, Inc.'s CEO, John Chambers, it was much better than that. He made $156 million from options and a mere $1.3 million from salary and bonuses in 2000. And that was when the company's stock was already down for the year.

According to Samuelson, ". . . stock options became corrupted by carelessness, overuse, and greed. As more executives developed big personal stakes in options, the task of keeping the stock price rising became separate from improving the business and its profitability." The March 4, 2002 *Business Week* magazine reported that from 1996 to 2000, the earnings of AOL/Time Warner would have been reduced 95% had it expensed options.

Can the existence of stock options cause stock prices to be manipulated?

A recent study suggests that options may motivate corporate executives to time announcements of good and bad news to maximize the value of their option grants. The study, published in *The Journal of Accounting and Economics* (Fall 2000), was conducted by Professor David Aboody of UCLA's Anderson Graduate School of Management, and Professor Ron Kasznik of Stanford's Graduate School of Business. Using SEC data covering 2039 options granted by 572 companies from 1992 to 1996, they found that the companies' stock prices hit their lowest on grant days. This was not a coincidence. "We find that the option grants are an incentive for CEOs to disclose bad news early and withhold good news," says Kasznik. Executives tend to disclose bad news before the grant, thereby, lowering their exercise price and announce good news after the grant is made.

Do stock options dilute corporate earnings?

Yes. According to an analyst's estimates, the reported earnings on the S & P 500 would be reduced by 50% when diluted by the exercise of existing options. John C. Bogle, founder of the Vanguard Funds, believes that stockholders are giving too much and getting too little for their money. Part of the problem, according to Mr. Bogle, is that when stock prices fall, management reprices the options to the lower price. This benefits management by temporarily depressing stock prices. In 1999, Mr. Bogle was concerned that repricing would result in a material dilution of earnings that could exacerbate any market decline. Was that a factor in 2000/2001? In any case, repricing has been severely restricted. **See Chapter Eight.**

Can the corporation be sued by its employees for stock options?

Yes. In fact, Eric Talley, University of Southern California Law School professor, says stock option proliferation has ". . . opened up the litigation floodgates." Six former Qualcomm employees sued the company in 1999 alleging fraud and breach of contract over the loss of stock options after Qualcomm sold its wireless division to Ericsson. The 1400 employees who lost their jobs at Qualcomm lost options valued at more than $500 million! Cisco Systems was also sued by a former employee of a company it had acquired. The employee had terminated, but believed that Cisco should honor his options with the company it acquired. Oracle Corporation was sued in May, 2000, by a former executive vice president. He claimed that he was fired six months before his retirement making him ineligible for options on 225,000 shares valued at $16 million. With this kind of money at stake we can expect more lawsuits over stock options.

It is not our position to argue the merits of any of these suits. Suffice it to say that the more clearly the option terms can be spelled out in advance, the better it will be for the corporation and the employee.

Avoiding Lawsuits

Both employers and employees can take a few simple steps to avoid litigation over stock options, employment lawyers say.

First, be as precise as possible in drafting option agreements. Spell out clearly when options will be vested, what happens when there is a change in corporate control, what constitutes an voluntary and involuntary departure, and under what if any circumstances an employee can exercise options after leaving the company.

A common mistake that employers make, says San Francisco attorney Garry Mathiason, is to base vesting on an employee's "anniversary date" without specifying that the employee must remain employed there in order for options to vest. Such a provision might allow employees to argue that they continued having 'anniversaries" even after they were no longer employed.

If an employee is to be fired or laid off close to the date a significant number of his options vest, then the employer should document precisely the reason for the firing or layoff. And similarly, corporate directors and officers can avoid personal liability by amply documenting the corporation's reason for termination.

-Margaret A. Jacobs
Wall Street Journal 4/12/01

Can anything be done to curb the abuse and save stock options for employees?

Prior to Enron, there was already a great deal of attention being given to some of the problems with stock options. In 2000, FASB changed its accounting rules requiring companies to take a charge against earnings for the cost of repricing options.

Additionally, shareholders started to object with 22% of shareholders voting against option plans in 2000. According to the Investor Responsibility Research Center in Washington, 10 plans were killed by shareholders in 2000, compared to just three in 1997. In December 2001, the SEC adapted new rules (effective March 15, 2002) requiring far greater disclosure of corporate stock option plans. Under the new rules, companies will have to disclose stock option plans that have not been approved by shareholders and, in many cases, are not accounted for on corporate proxy statements. Stock-based compensation plans that apply to a broad group of employees do not require shareholder approval. However, there was a lot of room for interpretation and non-approved plans have seen a six-fold increase according to a study done by iQuantic, Inc. **See Chapter Eight.**

By the time you read this, Congress may have devised a solution to the problem based upon the Enron hearings. In the meantime, *Newsweek's* Samuelson makes some good recommendations.

1. Change the accounting: count options as a cost. Currently, options are not a charge to earnings. See "Are Stock Options Chargeable to Corporate Earnings?" in this chapter. According to one accounting technique, Enron's options would have required deductions of about $2.4 billion from 1998 to 2000. That would have essentially eliminated the company's profit.

2. Index stock options to the market: If a company's stock price rises with the market, that doesn't necessarily reflect any management expertise. Executives, and other employees, should only be rewarded if they add value for the shareholders.

3. <u>Don't reprice options if the stock price falls:</u> Options are supposed to encourage executives to add value, in order to make the company grow. Why profit then if it falls? The shareholders certainly don't have this protection from bad management, why should the managers? The new FASB rules make this more difficult.

Chapter Three

What Are Nonqualified Stock Options?

What are Nonqualified Stock Options?

    Nonqualified stock option (NQSO) plans are the most popular form of stock option plans. In spite of the less desirable tax consequences, they offer substantially greater flexibility, thus their popularity. There is no limit on the dollar amount or number of shares that may be granted to an employee. Grants may be made to owners of more than 10% of the stock. NQSOs are taxed at the time of exercise at the same rate as your regular employee compensation.

How is my option price determined?

    Your option price is determined based upon the value of your company's stock on the day your stock option is granted. For example, if on the day the company grants your options, the share price in the market, or as determined by formula or appraisal (if there is no market price) is $10, then your exercise price is $10.

When can I exercise my option?

Your option needs to vest before you can exercise (buy the stock). Your company will usually set the vesting schedule at anywhere from one to five years. In some cases, the company will set a graded vesting schedule. For example, 20% after one year and 20% each additional year.

How long do I have to exercise my option?

Usually, NQSOs can be exercised after they vest for up to ten years after the grant date. Should you terminate employment, you usually will have only three months to exercise any vested options. In the event of death or disability, you may have a year or longer. Be sure to check your plan for specifics.

What happens when I exercise a Nonqualified Stock Option?

When you exercise your NQSOs, you are subject to ordinary income tax rates, income tax withholding, FICA, Medicare, and state and local income taxes. In other words, it is just as if your employer has given you additional income equal to the **spread**. The spread is the difference between your exercise price and the fair market value (FMV).

What do you mean by "exercise an option?"

When you exercise options, you exchange your right to purchase shares for a specific price for the actual shares of the company. You must pay the option price and the payroll taxes associated with your exercise.

Will I owe taxes when I exercise my options?

Yes. **See Chapter Six.**

What happens when I sell the stock I obtained from an NQSO?

When you sell your stock, you will be subject to either short or long-term capital gains on the difference between your exercise price and the sales price. **See Chapter Six.**

Example 3.1 Your option price was $10/share and the market price at execution was $20/share. You paid ordinary income taxes on the spread of $10/share, so your basis is $20/share. You now sell the stock for $50/share. Your taxable gain would be $30/share. Your tax would either be at 20% if you held the stock for more than a year (long-term capital gains), or at your ordinary income tax rates if you held for less than a year after exercising the option (short-term capital gains).

Can I exercise my options before they are vested?

Yes. If your company's plan allows for it, you may exercise your options before your stated vesting date. Usually this is done to reduce the amount subject to ordinary income when a substantial increase in stock price is anticipated. For example, before an IPO. When exercising early, the employee must make a Section 83(b) election. This is described later in this chapter.

Why should I exercise early?

Remember that NQSOs are subject to ordinary income and payroll taxes on the spread at the time of exercise. If you exercise before the IPO, you will pay less in taxes. Let's say that your option price is $10 and your company's stock is currently at $30. Your company is planning an IPO at $60 and analysts think it will be a hot offering reaching $100 or more. Your options won't vest until after the IPO. **See Table 3.1.**

Table 3.1	Pre IPO	Post IPO
Option price	$10	$10
Stock price	$30	$100
Spread	$20	$90
Tax @ 30%	$6	$27
Payroll taxes (FICA, etc.)	$2	$9
Total taxes	$8	$36

What is a Section 83(b) election?

Since an early election is still subject to the vesting requirements and may be repurchased by the corporation if you do not meet the vesting requirements, early exercise does not remove the substantial risk of forfeiture that would cause the option to be a taxable event. Therefore, you must make a conscious decision to be taxed at the time you make the early election, that is an 83(b) election. You thereby reduce the ordinary income tax consequences and start the time running for capital gains treatment on your subsequent sale.

What happens if I have made an 83(b) election and sell the stock once it vests, but before one year after exercise?

This would be a short-term capital gain and subject to ordinary income tax. However, it would not be subject to additional payroll taxes. This could provide a significant savings to you. **See Chapter Six.**

Chapter Four

What Are Incentive Stock Options?

What is an Incentive Stock Option?

Incentive stock options (ISOs) are also known as **statutory stock options** because they are subject to a strict set of statutory regulations. They offer significantly better tax benefits than nonqualified stock options. All options are granted as an incentive, they are often all referred to as ISOs or incentive stock options. You must determine which type of option you actually have because the benefits and restrictions will be different.

ISOs are subject to a written plan set out and approved by the company's board of directors and stockholders. The plan must list the employees who are eligible and the number of shares available to grant to employees. ISOs have a fixed expiry date of ten years. The price of the option is set the date the option is granted and must be the fair market value (FMV) of the stock as of that date. The employee may not transfer the option.

Are there restrictions on granting ISOs?

A company granting ISOs must be careful to comply with the statutory requirements of IRS Section 422 if it is to gain the tax benefits associated with ISOs. In addition to the written plan approved by the board of directors and stockholders, the company can only issue incentive stock options to employees who own less than 10% of the voting power of the company. You must be an employee of the company at the time the option is granted and at all times up to within three months of the date of exercise (one year if disabled). The options cannot be transferred. The company cannot grant more than $100,000 of qualified options that are exercisable in the same year to any one employee. While offering better tax benefits to the employee than non-statutory plans, these plans are less popular because of their many restrictions.

What happens if my employer grants more than $100,000 of ISOs to me that are exercisable in the same year?

While rare, it is possible that you could have more than $100,000 of options become exercisable in the same year (the $100,000 is on the option price, not the fair market value of the shares). IRC Section 422(d) specifies that the $100,000 is based on when the options become exercisable not when they are exercised. **See Example 4.1.** In such cases, the options in excess of $100,000 would be considered nonqualified stock options. **See Chapter Three.**

How is the price of my options determined?

The price of the options is set at the fair market value of the stock as of the date the options are issued. This usually is the price of the stock in the market or as determined by formula or appraisal on the date the options are granted to you.

Example 4.1 Your employer grants you ISOs valued at $50,000 in year one and requires a two year vesting. On the same date a year later, you receive a new option for $75,000 with only a one year vesting requirement. You would have $125,000 of options which would become exercisable at the same time. It would not matter whether you exercised none, some, or all of the options at that time. When you do exercise, only $100,000 will be treated as ISOs, the balance will be treated as NQSOs.

What happens when I exercise an Incentive Stock Option?

When ISOs are exercised, the difference between the fair market value of the stock and the exercise price of the option (the spread) results in income, according to IRC Section 83. While this income is not subject to ordinary income or payroll taxes, the spread is subject to AMT. *(This may change after December 31, 2002. If IRS Notice 2001-14 is implemented, payroll taxes will be due upon exercise.)* However, the spread is subject to the **alternative minimum tax** (AMT). Careful planning is required to minimize the tax consequences of exercising incentive stock options to avoid the AMT. **See Chapter Six.**

When can I sell my Incentive Stock Option shares?

As noted above, ISOs are subject to special rules. You are required to hold the shares from an ISO exercise at least two years from the date of issue of the option grant and one year from the date of exercise. Failure to do so, will result in the ISO being treated in the same fashion as a NQSO. **See Example 4.2.**

What happens when I sell the stock I obtained from exercising my ISO?

If you hold your stock for more than one year from the date of exercising the option and two years from the date of the grant, then your stock will be taxed at the long-term capital gains rate to the extent your sales price exceeds your exercise price. The spread was already subject to ordinary or AMT tax at the time of execution. Only the gain is now subject to tax.

Example 4.2 Usually ISOs are granted with a one year vesting requirement. If you exercise the option when it vests, then you will meet the two year grant and one year hold at the end of the second year and be eligible for ISO and long-term capital gains treatment. If you had a two year vest or if you did not exercise the option when it vested, then you would have to hold one year after exercise before sale to qualify for ISO treatment.

What happens if I sell my ISO shares at a loss?

If you sell your shares below the exercise price, you have a capital loss, either short or long-term, for regular tax purposes. However, your AMT tax may be different. **See Chapter Six.**

Can I exercise my ISO options early (before vesting)?

Yes, if your plan allows for it. This is the same as the Section 83(b) election discussed in Chapter Three. However, an early election and an 83(b) election will not trigger ordinary income taxes. Only the AMT is accelerated to the date of exercise.

May I gift my Incentive Stock Options to a family member or charity?

No. Incentive Stock Options are nontransferable.

May I gift the shares I acquired from exercising my Incentive Stock Options?

Yes. However if you have not met the holding period requirements, your gift will result in a disqualifying disposition the same as when you sell the stock too soon.

Chapter Five

What are Employee Stock Purchase Plans?

What are Employee Stock Purchase Plans?

Employee Stock Purchase Plans (ESPP) are programs sponsored by the employer to encourage employee ownership of company stock. The plans may be statutory qualifying under IRC Section 423 for special tax benefits or nonqualified and lacking tax benefits. Usually, the employee is able to obtain the employer's stock at a discount from the market price.

What is the difference between a Section 423 ESPP and a nonqualified ESPP?

A Section 423 Plan is qualified under the Code. If certain holding period requirements are met, the employee will not be subject to tax on the purchase of the stock and will receive long-term capital gains treatment on the sale. *(IRS Notice 2001-14 will require payroll withholding after December 31, 2002.)* Seventy-five percent of plans are 423 plans.

A nonqualified plan has similar provisions to the statutory plan, but does not meet the statutory requirements and, therefore, does not offer the employee any tax benefits. Both plans provide the employee with a discount, usually 15%, on the purchase of company stock.

A third plan is the **open market purchase plan**. This has no tax benefits and no discount. Usually the employer has made arrangements with a broker to allow for small purchases of the company's stock at a reduced commission cost.

How do Section 423 plans work?

Employees elect to have a percentage of compensation withheld from their paychecks each pay period on an after-tax basis. Periodically the company buys shares, typically at a price that is 85% of the lower of the stock's fair market value on the first day of the period or on the purchase date. In a rising market, the employee is obtaining a discount in excess of 15%. In a declining market, the employee benefits from the lower price. The spread is not recognized as income.

How is an ESPP different from a stock option plan?

ESPPs are generally available to all employees while stock options are given to selected classes of employees by the company. The amount of stock you purchase is determined by the amount of your deferral, not the number of options granted. In an ESPP you purchase at 85% of the market value; with stock options, the price is set at the time the option is granted.

What are the benefits of participation in my company's ESPP?

You are able to purchase your company's stock at a discount. You are able to dollar cost average into your employer's stock. The discount you receive is not subject to taxation provided that you meet the holding requirements.

Does my salary reduction reduce my income taxes?

No. Your ESPP deduction is with after-tax dollars. The advantage in a 423 plan is that you pay no taxes on the spread. In a nonqualified plan or open market plan, you have no tax advantage.

How much will I pay for stock purchased in the ESPP?

As mentioned above, the discount is usually 15% of the fair market value either on the date of purchase or the beginning of the period (sometimes known as the enrollment or grant date), whichever is lower.

Example when share price is rising:

Price at beginning date	$25.00
Price at purchase date	$30.00
Price for ESPP (25.00 x .85)	$21.25

Example when share price is falling:

Price at beginning date	$25.00
Price at purchase date	$20.00
Price for ESPP (20.00 x .85)	$17.00

Will the price always be at a discount?

Not necessarily. There is no requirement that shares be purchased at a discount, only a limitation on how much of a discount to qualify as an ESPP. Fifteen percent is the maximum.

May senior management and board members participate in the ESPP?

ESPPs are for employees only, so board members are out. Additionally, employees holding 5% or more of company stock are excluded. Other than that, senior management may participate, however, the plan may be drafted to specifically exclude "highly compensated" employees.

As an officer of the company, should I not participate in the company's ESPP because of Section 16 reporting requirements?

Section 16 should not preclude you from participating. No Section 16 reporting is required as a result of your election to participate, making contributions, changing your contribution, or withdrawing contributions before stock is purchased. Stock purchased through the ESPP is also exempt. If the ESPP distributes your stock to you, the transaction is exempt for short-swing profits liability purposes and no reporting is required.

However, you must report your ESPP holdings when filing Forms 4 and 5. You may want to footnote the source of the shares. Any sale of ESPP shares in the open market must be reported on Form 4. The sale is subject to short-swing profits liability the same as any other shares you might purchase. **See Chapter Twelve.**

How long do I have to hold ESPP shares to receive favorable tax treatment?

Like ISOs, you must hold ESPP shares for one year after the purchase date and two years after the grant (enrollment) date.

If I sell my shares before the end of the holding period, what will be the tax consequence?

If you sell your shares within two years of grant or one year of purchase, you will have ordinary income for the difference between the purchase price and the fair market value of the stock on the purchase date. Even if the lower price at time of grant was used, you will still use the FMV at time of purchase to determine your tax liability. You will also have a capital gain or loss on the difference as of the date you sold the stock from the FMV at the date of purchase. Note that if the stock has gone down but exceeds the discount price you payed, you would still have ordinary income. Currently, your employer would not withhold taxes. *(IRS Notice 2001-14, if implemented, will require withholding post December 31, 2002.)*

May I give away or exchange my shares prior to the end of the holding period?

This would also be considered a disqualifying disposition and subject you to tax. See above.

Does the Alternative Minimum Tax apply to ESPPs?

No. The AMT only applies to Incentive Stock Options.

Are there any securities law restrictions on the purchase or sale of ESPP stock?

As noted above, since an ESPP is a plan that is not controlled by the executive, it is exempt from the rules and regulations under Section 16. However, all employees are subject to insider trading rules. If you are aware of information about your company that has not been made public, you may not sell your shares until that information has been publicly disclosed.

Chapter Six

What About Taxes On Stock Options?

General Rules on Option Taxation

What are the income tax rules for stock options?

IRC Section 83 provides that a taxpayer who receives property as compensation for services rendered must recognize the value of that property as income when the property becomes transferable or when there is no longer a substantial risk of forfeiture, whichever occurs first. The income recognized is the excess of the fair market value (determined without regard to restrictions that will never lapse) over the amount paid for such property by the taxpayer. This is the **spread**.

If the stock option does not have a readily ascertainable fair market value (FMV), the grant of the option does not result in the recognition of income under IRC Section 83. IRC Section 83 does not cause recognition of income with respect to the option until the date of exercise, even if the option attains a readily ascertainable FMV in the interim. When options are exercised, the issuance of the stock results in ordinary income equal to the spread at the time of the exercise.

Do I recognize income when my employer grants me a stock option?

Generally not. IRC Section 83 provides that a taxpayer who receives property as compensation for services rendered must recognize the value of the property as income when the property is transferred or when there is no longer a substantial risk of forfeiture, whichever occurs first. The income recognized is the excess of the FMV of the property over the amount paid for the property by the taxpayer. Section 83 provides that if the option does not have a readily ascertainable fair market value, then the grant does not result in the recognition of income. Generally, a stock option does not have a readily ascertainable fair market value, therefore, the grant of the option does not result in the recognition of income under IRC Section 83. The option won't result in the recognition of income until it is exercised. Even if the option subsequently attains a readily ascertainable FMV, it will not result in taxable income until exercised.

What is the tax on the sale of NQSOs?

When you exercise NQSOs the spread is generally taxed at ordinary income rates in that year. Your employer will add the spread to your W-2 taxable income along with all the usual payroll taxes. Your basis in the shares is the market price on the exercise date. If you subsequently sell for less than the market price on the exercise date, you have a capital loss. **See Example 6.1.**

If you die with outstanding NQSOs, your estate or beneficiaries can exercise the options subject to ordinary income taxes, but not W-2 income subject to payroll taxes.

> **Example 6.1** On June 30, 2000, you receive an NQSO giving you the right to purchase 100 shares of employer stock for $10/share. You exercise on June 30, 2001, when the market price is $16/share. Your spread is $600 (FMV $16 - OP $10 = S $6). You will pay 2001 taxes on the $600 spread at your ordinary rate plus payroll taxes. The taxes will be owed to your employer at the time of exercise.

Suppose I quit and move to another state, what is the tax on my NQSOs?

Your employment status is determined at the time you receive the options. Even though you are no longer employed at the time of exercise, you will be subject to W-2 taxes. Most states will tax you based upon your state of residence at the time of the grant. You will not escape taxes by moving.

I am a consultant/board member not subject to W-2, how am I taxed?

Since you are not an employee, the company is not responsible for withholding for you. Instead, your income based on the spread will be reported on your Form 1099 at the end of the year. You will be responsible for the taxes. Employment status is determined at the time of the grant so if you subsequently become an employee, you will have to separate your pre-employment and post-employment options since they will be taxed differently. You are not eligible for ISOs since they are only available to employees who own less than 10% of the stock of the company.

What is a Section 83(b) election?

Suppose you have options at $1 per share and your stock is at $5 per share. Your options won't vest for another six months, but your company is going public and the market price is expected to hit $20 per share. Your company may allow you to exercise your options in advance, subject to delayed vesting and other restrictions. In other words, you will receive restricted stock. As the shares remain subject to a risk of forfeiture, the exercise does not automatically trigger a taxable event.

You must make a Section 83(b) election to be taxed on the exercise of the options while they are still subject to a substantial risk of forfeiture.

Why should I make an 83(b) election?

Using the example above: if you wait until your options vest to exercise and your company's stock is now trading at $20, then your spread will be $19 ($20 - $1). You will be paying ordinary income taxes and payroll taxes on this amount times the number of shares you exercise. However, by exercising early your spread is only $4 ($5 - $1). Your taxes are only about 20% of what they would have been.

Are there any risks to an 83(b) election?

Yes. If the stock doesn't rise in value, you have accelerated your tax liability. If the stock drops in value, your spread would be lower resulting in less tax. If you terminate employment before vesting, you may have your shares repurchased or forfeited.

I exercised my options early and filed an 83(b) election. I'm terminating employment before vesting. How do I file for the tax loss?

You don't. You probably planned on things being different when you filed your 83(b) election; you had incurred payroll taxes in hopes of reducing your future tax liability. If your former employer is now buying back your stock, it is probably at the option price. In this case, you have no loss. You paid $1,000 for the stock and you are getting $1,000 back.

If the shares were worth $5000 at the time you filed the 83(b) election, you recognized $4000 as income on the spread. Unfortunately, there is no provision in the law to allow you to recover the payroll taxes on the $4000. If the company requires you to forfeit your shares, then you can at least claim the $1000 you paid as a capital loss (probably short-term).

How do I file an 83(b) election?

Your election must be filed with your company in writing within 30 days of when you exercise the option. This also starts the clock on your holding period for long-term capital gains. A copy of the 83(b) election must also be filed with your tax return for the year. **See Example 6.2.**

Incentive Stock Option Taxation

What are the "Regular Tax" rules for the sale of ISO shares?

If you have ISOs, you will get two regular tax advantages (as opposed to AMT). First, when you exercise at a price below the market value on the exercise date, the spread is not currently taxed under the regular tax rules.

Second, when you eventually sell your ISOs, the entire profit can qualify for the 20% maximum rate on long-term capital gains. This applies only when you sell the ISOs more than two years after the option grant date (the date you received the option) and more than one year after you actually bought the shares by exercising your ISOs. **See Example 6.3.**

Example 6.2
Sample Section 83(b) Election

The undersigned hereby elects pursuant to Section 83(b) of the Internal Revenue Code to be taxed in the current year on the property described below:

1. The name, address and taxpayer identification number of the undersigned is: <u>Bill Smith, 1234 Elm St., Anytown, USA 10001 TIN 000-00-0000</u>
2. Description of property with respect to this election: <u>1000 shares of Common Stock, par value $1 per share, of ABC Co.</u>
3. The date on which property was transferred: <u>July 1, 2002</u>
4. The taxable year for this election: <u>2002</u>
5. The nature of the restriction to which the property is subject: <u>Should my employment terminate prior to January 1, 2003, for any reason other than death or disability, I must forfeit the subject shares to ABC Co. without value.</u>
6. Fair Market Value: <u>The fair market value of the shares at the time of transfer were determined by company formula to be $5 per share.</u>
7. Amount paid for the property: <u>$1000 (based upon $1 per share option price)</u>
8. A copy of this statement has been filed with the employee and ABC Co.

Date: _____   Signed: _____

Example 6.3 On June 30, 2000, you received an ISO giving you the right to purchase 100 shares of employer stock for $10/share. You exercised on June 30, 2001, when the market price was $16/share. Your per share basis is $10 (exercise price). You sell on July 1, 2002, for $25/share. The sale date is more than two years after the June 30, 2000, grant date and more than 12 months after the June 30, 2001, exercise date. Therefore, your entire $1,500 profit is treated as a long-term capital gain qualifying for the 20% rate.

What happens if I sell my ISOs at a loss?

Generally, if you sell shares below the exercise price, you have a capital loss either short or long term for regular tax purposes. However, you may have different consequences if you were subject to the AMT on exercise.

If you sold your shares in the same year as you exercised your options, then you have a **disqualifying disposition**. This would cancel the AMT calculation and result in the exercise of the options being taxed at ordinary rates, but no payroll taxes *(IRS Notice 2001-14, if implemented will require withholding post December 31, 2002)* and then a short-term gain or loss on the stock depending on your exercise price and sale price. If the stock has dropped significantly, as has happened with many companies in recent years, this may be a desirable option. **See Example 6.4.**

Example 6.4 You exercise your option in 2001 for $10/share when the stock is selling for $30/share. You are subject to AMT on the $20/share spread. Now the stock has dropped to $15/share. For regular tax purposes, you will have a gain of $5/share short or long-term depending on your holding period. For AMT purposes, you would have a loss of $15/share ($30/share market value at execution - $15/share value at sale). This would show up as a "negative adjustment" on your Form 6251. If you paid AMT in 2001, then you would have an AMT credit to apply against your regular income tax.

What is the Alternative Minimum Tax?

The **Alternative Minimum Tax** (AMT) is like an entirely separate tax system. It eliminates most of the deductions and imposes a different tax rate table. It was instituted to catch individuals who were not paying taxes as a result of various tax shelters. In 1970, only 19,000 tax payers owed the AMT. By 1996, about 600,000 taxpayers got caught by the AMT. Because the AMT is not indexed, it is estimated that more than 8.4 million taxpayers will pay the AMT in 2007! Generally, if your gross income exceeds $75,000 and you have any write-offs for personal exemptions, taxes, and home-equity loan interest, then you will need to complete Form 6251, the AMT calculation.

To calculate the AMT you must first determine your taxable income on Form 1040. Then you add back your personal and dependent exemptions; your standard deduction; state, local, foreign, and property tax write-offs; and home-equity loan interest if the proceeds were not used for home improvement. Then you lose most of your itemized deductions such as investment expenses, employee business expenses, and medical and dental expenses. Finally, if you exercised an ISO, you add in the spread. Now that you have calculated your AMT income, you are allowed to apply the AMT exemption, $45,000 joint or $33,750 single. The deduction is lost at $.25 per dollar of AMT income over $150,000 joint or $112,500 single income. After the exemption (if any), the tax rate is 26% on the first $175,000 and 28% on the excess.

Once the AMT and regular tax are determined, the taxpayer is required to pay the larger amount. While much attention is given to avoiding the AMT, for many executives with ISOs, the AMT is simply a fact of life.

What are the AMT rules?

For AMT purposes, your tax basis equals the market price on the exercise date, rather than the lower exercise price. This shows up as a "negative adjustment" when you sell. So, if you eventually sell for less than the market price on the exercise date, you'll have an AMT loss (although you'll still have a regular tax gain when the sale price exceeds the exercise price). If you end up selling for more than the market price on the exercise date, your AMT gain will still be lower than your regular tax profit. In either case, if you earned an AMT credit in the exercise year and still haven't used it, you may be able to use it to reduce your tax when you sell. **See Example 6.5.**

Example 6.5 The facts are the same as in *Example 6.1*. For 2001 AMT purposes, you reported a $600 positive adjustment (the spread on the exercise date) on Form 6251 (Alternative Minimum Tax – Individuals). Your per share basis for AMT purposes is $16 (market value on the exercise date). When you prepare your 2002 return, complete IRS Form 8801 (Credit for Prior Year Minimum Tax) to see if you qualify for an AMT credit. On your 2002 Form 6251 you'll report a $600 negative adjustment to account for the difference between regular tax and AMT basis in your shares so your AMT gain will be only $900. If you have any AMT credit, you'll probably be able to use it to reduce your 2002 tax. Any leftover credit gets carried over to 2003.

What is the AMT credit?

The AMT credit comes from incurring AMT taxes due to temporary AMT preference items. The exercise of an ISO is the key temporary preference item. Permanent items would include itemized deductions, state and local taxes, and property taxes. While triggering AMT, permanent items do not create an AMT credit. The exercise of an ISO results in a temporary preference creating an AMT credit that may be used to reduce taxes in subsequent years. To the extent that your AMT tax is below your regular tax in the year of the sale of the stock, you may apply the credit to your regular tax. AMT credit is lost at death. Planning for the AMT credit is one of the reasons that you should seek expert advice before the exercise of your options.

What happens when I sell the stock if I had to pay AMT tax on the exercise?

The AMT tax on ISOs qualifies for an AMT credit. Therefore, at the time you sell the stock, you need to complete Form 8801 to see if you qualify for the AMT credit. Additionally, since you had to pay taxes on the spread, your basis in the stock for capital gains tax purposes is the market value at the time you exercised the option, not the option price. **See Table 6.1.**

Table 6.1

Example of AMT Calculation

Regular Tax Calculation		AMT Calculation	
Salary/Int./Divid.	$255,000	Item deduction add back	
Taxes	16,000	Taxes	$16,000
Deductible Int.	15,000	Misc. deductions	5,000
Contributions	6,000	ISO preference	50,000
Misc. deductions	5,000	Less: phase out	(3,765)
Total deductions	42,000	Alt. taxable income	279,000
Less: phase out	(3,765)	Less: exemption	(12,750)
Net itemized ded.	38,235	Subject to AMT	266,250
Reg. taxable inc.	211,765	Tax @ 26%: 175,000	45,500
		Tax @ 28%: 91,250	25,550
Regular tax	57,997	Total tentative AMT	61,050
		Add. AMT tax	3,053

Is there any way to avoid or reduce the AMT?

In order to avoid the AMT, you must keep your income below the AMT threshold. You can reduce your potential for the

AMT by minimizing the spread when exercising your options. Therefore, you may want to exercise your options soon after they vest. If the stock has already substantially appreciated, you may want to stagger your exercises over a period of several years. Of course, you will have to watch the expiry date.

If you are not able to manage your option income, you may be able to reduce other AMT income items to avoid the AMT. For example, you may be able to defer part of your income, such as a bonus, until the following year. You may want to defer exercising your ISOs until the end of the year. This gives you a chance to see what happens with your company's stock. Perhaps the price will drop, reducing your spread and eliminating the potential for the AMT. Alternatively, if you think your company's stock may be going down, you may want to exercise your ISOs early in the year. Should the share price drop during the year, you sell your shares acquired by exercising your ISOs before the end of the year you exercised in. This will result in a disqualifying disposition which will result in your option being taxed at ordinary income rates with no AMT. You would pay ordinary income taxes, but avoid a loss when the market price drop below your option price.

You may want to use your money to buy another company's stock rather than exercise your ISOs. If you don't exercise, you won't have any AMT.

Why would I want to use my money to buy another stock rather than "take down" my options?

Suppose it would take $20,000 to exercise your options, instead you invest the $20,000 in another company. Assume that your company and the other company appreciate at the same rate for three years. At the end of three years, the other company's stock is worth $25,000, you sell, realize a profit of $5,000, and pay a capital gains tax (20% or $1,000). This leaves you with a net gain of $4,000. Now you take your $20,000 and exercise your options. Remember that your option price is fixed until the option expires. Therefore, while the stock price has increased over the three years, your cost to exercise has not. Now your company's stock is worth $27,500. You sell the stock the next day, a disqualifying disposition, resulting in ordinary income tax. At 40%, your tax is $3,000. You net $4,500 on the option and $4,000 on the other company for a total after-tax-return of $8,500. Had you exercised the option to begin with and been fortunate enough to avoid the AMT, your net gain would have been $6,000 (80% of the $7,500 gain). Of course, the other company's stock has to have a reasonable return in order for this to work.

The point is, it is not always necessary to rush in and exercise your ISOs the moment they vest. Your employer is basically making you an interest free loan until you exercise.

What will trigger the AMT?

Ernst & Young gives the following examples of the amount of AMT adjustments (ISO spread, state and local taxes, other AMT adjustments) that, when added back to regular income, are likely to trigger the payment of the AMT for the year. **See Table 6.2.**

Table 6.2

Regular taxable income	Joint return AMT items	Single return AMT items
$50,000	$26,924	$24,472
100,000	30,770	28,518
150,000	31,758	28,888
200,000	33,284	31,075

What is a disqualifying disposition?

A **disqualifying disposition** is when you violate either of the two ISO holding rules of the IRC. You sell or transfer the stock either within two years of the grant date or within one year of the exercise date.

What are the tax consequences of a disqualifying disposition?

A disqualifying disposition has both regular tax and AMT consequences. When the sale price exceeds the exercise price, you have a regular tax gain. That means the gain, up to the amount of the spread at the time of exercise, is treated as compensation income when you sell the shares. However, no payroll tax withholding is required. *(IRS Notice 2001-14, if enacted, will require withholding for tax years after December 31, 2002.)* This ordinary income piece of the gain is taxed at your regular rate. Any additional gain is long or short-term capital gain. The rate on the capital gain piece depends on your holding period which begins on the exercise date. When your sale price is below the exercise price, you have a capital loss for regular tax purposes (short-term capital loss if you held the shares for a year or less and long-term capital loss otherwise). If you make a disqualifying disposition by selling less than two years after the grant date but you owned the shares for more than a year after the exercise date, the capital gain element would qualify for the 20% capital gains tax.

Is there any other way to reduce or eliminate my taxes when exercising an ISO?

Perhaps. If you are an insider, an officer, or hold 10% or more of the company's stock, you may be an "affiliated person" under the terms of the Securities Act of 1933, Rule 144. If so, your stock will be restricted. You will have to hold the stock for one year from the date of exercising your option. In this case, you may qualify for a discount on the market value of your stock at the time you exercise your option. You will need a professional appraiser to determine just how much of a discount you are eligible for.

The idea here is that since you cannot legally sell the stock at the point you exercise it, it is subject to market risks that you have no control over. If you fit into this category, then a few thousand dollars spent on an appraisal may save you many times that amount in taxes and you might possibly avoid the AMT. However, this is a questionable position and should not be undertaken without the advice of expert tax counsel. **See Chapter Thirteen.**

May I make an 83(b) election for my ISOs?

Yes. You may make a special Section 83(b) election for ISOs similar to an 83(b) election for NQSOs. See the questions on 83(b) elections earlier in the chapter.

When is the best time to exercise my ISOs?

In Chapter Seven, I suggested that you might want to wait until later in the year to exercise your ISOs. This would give you a chance to evaluate the impact of and perhaps avoid the AMT. However, if you exercise late in the year, you may have a more significant problem than paying some additional taxes. As the market correction of 2000/2001 demonstrated, stock prices don't always go up. A disqualifying disposition takes place if you don't meet the one year/two year requirements, so you must sell the stock in the same year as the year of exercise if you are to avoid the AMT.

Why would I want to do that?

Let's make it easy:

You exercise 10000 shares at $10 when the market value is $60. The $50 spread creates a preference item for the AMT of $500,000 and a tax liability of $150,000. Now, as in 2000 and 2001, your company's stock falls and the price is $12 when it comes time to pay your taxes. You sell all of your shares and still are $30,000 short of the taxes due.

Gifting of Stock Options

Am I subject to income on the options if I make a gift of them?

No. IRC Section 83 does not require you to recognize income for compensation purposes until the value of the income is readily determinable. Until the option is exercised, its value cannot be determined. You have reduced your taxable estate without having to pay the income tax at the time of the gift. Remember, you cannot gift ISOs.

When the option is exercised, who recognizes the income?

Only the employee is subject to income taxes. (IRC Section 83) The beneficiaries have merely received the options as a gift. They did not perform services for the employer. When the recipient exercises the option, the employee or donor will have to pay all the payroll taxes.

Is there a way to retain the income tax consequences while making a completed gift for estate tax purposes?

A grantor trust, under sub-chapter J, allows the grantor to obtain all of the tax consequences (income and deductions) of the trust. To qualify as a grantor trust, the grantor must retain certain powers over the trust. These include: the right of the grantor to reacquire trust property by substitution; the power held by a non-adverse party to control the beneficial enjoyment by beneficiaries; the power to borrow from the trust without adequate security; and actually borrowing from the trust. While incomplete for income tax purposes, the gift will be complete for estate tax purposes.

Why would I want to retain the income tax consequences?

By retaining the income tax consequences, you will pay both Section 83 income taxes on the exercise (required) and the capital gains taxes on the sale of the stock. You will, thereby, further reduce your taxable estate by the amount of the taxes as well as the gift of the stock.

Won't this strategy result in an additional taxable gift?

Maybe, but maybe not. Section 83(b) income belongs to the donor and is not subject to gift taxes. However, the capital gains tax under a sub-chapter J trust is less clear. In PLR 9444033, the IRS found that such an arrangement did constitute an additional gift. However, in PLR 9543049, the IRS reversed its position without explanation or comment. Since PLR 9543049 is more recent, it is viewed as the IRS's current position. However, private letter rulings (PLR) only apply to the specific case and situation for which they were issued and are not binding on the IRS.

Taxes on Publicly Traded Stock Options

While they are not part of the employer grant options addressed in this book, we will include a few items on **traded options** since they may be part of your overall investment plan and can, in some cases, be used in conjunction with ISOs and NQSOs.

If you hold options, they will either: (1) expire unexercised on the expiration date because they are worthless, (2) be exercised because they are "in the money" or (3) be sold before they expire.

If your options expire, you have obviously sustained a capital loss, usually short-term. For example, you buy a six-month **call option** with a strike price of $20/share. On the expiration date, the stock is selling for $10/share. You let the options expire and, thereby, incur a short-term capital loss (the cost of the option).

If you sell your options, things are simple. You have a capital gain or loss that is either short-term or long-term, depending on your holding period.

Option writers (sellers) receive premiums for their efforts. The receipt of the premium has no tax consequences for the writer until the option: (1) expires unexercised, (2) is exercised or (3) is offset in a **closing transaction**. In a closing transaction, you sell an option that is identical to the option you hold. If the premium you receive exceeds your cost basis, you have a capital gain. If the premium is less than your cost basis, you have a capital loss.

When a put or call expires, you treat the premium payment as a short-term capital gain realized on the expiration date. This is true even if the duration of the option exceeds twelve months.

If you own a **put option** that gets exercised (meaning you have to buy the stock), then you reduce the tax basis of the shares you acquire by the premium you paid. Again, your holding period starts the day after you acquire the shares.

If you write a call option that gets exercised (meaning you sell the stock), add the premium to the sales proceeds. Your gain or loss is short-term or long-term, depending on how long you hold the shares. **See Example 6.6.**

If you have an **offsetting position** with respect to the option, your tax benefits may be deferred. For example, you buy a put option on appreciated stock you already own, but are precluded from selling it currently under SEC rules. Say the put option expires near the end of the year. If you still own the offsetting position (the stock) at year's end, your loss from the expired option is generally deductible only to the extent that it exceeds the unrealized gain on the stock. Any excess loss is deferred until the year you sell the stock.

Example 6.6 You spend $300 on a July 17, 2001, call option to buy 300 shares of Fast Growth, Inc., at $15/share. On July 17, it's selling for $35/share, so you exercise. Add the $300 option cost to the $4,500 spent on the shares (300 times $15). Your basis in the stock is $4800, and your holding period begins on July 18, the day after you acquire the shares.

Are there any special concerns about state taxes?

One of the biggest questions is, which state do you get taxed in? Say your first grant is made in New York, your in Texas, and they vest when you are in California. Then you retire in Nevada and exercise your options. Which state collects the taxes? Here are a few points from California to serve as an example.

Move in and exercise: California taxes the spread because the income is recognized in the state.

Move out and exercise: California taxes the spread because the option was earned in the state.

Non-resident with some work in the state: California allocates the share of work in the state to determine the tax.

California has its own rules for ISOs. R&TC Section 17502.

Public Law 104-95 prohibits states from taxing retirement income of non-residents. It doesn't apply to stock options. Seek expert advice.

Chapter Seven

How Do I Exercise My Stock Options?

What if I don't have the money to exercise my stock options?

There are still several ways that you may exercise your options. You could consider postponing the exercise to a later time when you have had a chance to accumulate the funds to pay the exercise price. Of course, you run the risk of paying more taxes on a higher spread at that time. You need to make sure that you watch the expiry date of your options. Your employer may have a program where it will lend you money to exercise your options. Most brokerage firms also have a program where they will lend money against the stock you will be acquiring. This is a margin loan. You may have other stock that you can sell or margin against as well. Of course, if you borrow to buy, you may have to sell some shares to cover your debt. If the shares you borrow against are ISOs and the sale is within one year, then the sale would be a disqualifying distribution.

What is a cashless exercise?

A **cashless exercise** requires you to exercise options and sell some of the acquired shares to cover the cost of the options and the taxes due. This is for both NQSOs and ISOs. However, it is a disqualifying distribution for the ISOs. Frequently, all shares are sold in a cashless option. However, you may want to sell only enough shares to cover the cost of the options and taxes and hold the balance for one year to get long-term capital gains treatment.

What is a Stock Swap?

If you own other stock from your employer, perhaps from a prior option exercise, you may be able to swap those shares for your option shares (IRC Section 422(c)(4)(A)). The stock swap will leverage the appreciation in your existing shares and defer any tax liability on the swap. The tax deferral reduces the cost basis on your newly acquired shares. If the market value is above your exercise price, you will be increasing your number of shares without an out of pocket expense. **See Example 7.1.**

Can I do a Stock Swap on ISOs as well?

Yes, but there are some issues. If your existing shares were acquired through the exercise of ISOs or through an ESPP, then you must meet the holding requirements. The swap, while a tax free exchange, is still a disposition of the original shares and would be disqualifying if the holding period was not met. Because income is calculated differently for regular tax and AMT for ISOs, you will get different results for the two calculations. Using Example 7.1 and in accordance with IRS Private Letter Ruling (PLR) 9629028 you have the results in **Example 7.2**.

Example 7.1 On January 31, 2000, you did a cashless exercise on 2500 shares of your company stock at a current market price of $20 per share and an exercise price of $10 per share. You sold 1500 shares generating $30,000 which covered the $25,000 exercise cost and your $5,000 tax liability. You now hold 1000 shares. You want to exercise 1000 newly vested options at $20 per share, and the stock is now at $50. Your exercise cost is $20,000 ($20 per share x 1000 shares). You "swap" 400 shares of your current holdings at the market price (400 x $50 = $20,000) for the new 1000 shares. There is no gain recognized on the "swap" of your old shares. The transfer qualifies as a stock-for-stock tax deferred exchange under IRC Section 1036.

You do recognize income on the exercise of an NQSO. In this case, you would have ordinary compensation of $30,000 ($50,000 FMV - $20,000 exercise cost). In accordance with Rev. Rule 80-244 and IRC Section 1223, your basis and holding period would be: 400 shares would have the original basis of $10 per share and a holding period from January 31, 2000. The remaining 600 shares would have a basis of $30,000 or $20 per share.

Example 7.2	**Swap Shares**	**New Shares**
Regular Tax:		
Basis: 400 shares - $10/share		600 shares - $0/share
Holding Period: Jan. 31, 2000		date of exercise
AMT:		
Basis: 400 shares - $10/share		600 shares - $20/share
Holding Period: date of exercise		date of exercise

Do I sell my stock for the stock swap?

No. In essence, you are swapping shares on the company's books, your old shares in exchange for the new shares. In PLR 9629028, the IRS ruled that, in lieu of actually transferring to the company, the option holder could make a constructive exchange of shares. In other words, if your shares are with a broker, you get a notarized statement attesting to the number of shares held and your intent to use the shares as payment. If you hold the shares, you provide the employer with the certificate numbers. The company treats your shares as being constructively received and issues new shares for the difference. For example, you use 100 existing shares to exercise 1000 options. You keep your 100 shares and the company issues 900 new shares. Your tax consequences is on the 1000 shares.

Why would I want to do a stock swap?

A stock swap allows you to exercise your options on a cashless basis while realizing the gain in your current shares without paying tax. You have a tax deferred exchange in accordance with IRC Section 1036. If your company reloads your options you must use your existing company stock to qualify. **See Reload Feature.**

May I use a margin loan to exercise my options?

Brokers are allowed by Regulation T of the Federal Reserve to lend up to 50% of a stock's value on the date of the loan. This is called a **margin loan**. The broker can set a lower percent on certain stocks or not grant margin lending on a stock. If your broker will lend you money on your company's stock, then you can make the purchase with a margin loan. If the company's stock price is two or more times the price of your option on the date of exercise and the broker granted a 50% margin loan, then you could purchase the stock without cash. While you will have to pay the margin interest expense, you will be able to hold the stock for one year and get long-term capital gains treatment when you sell the stock and pay off your margin loan. Of course, if the price of the stock drops, you may have a margin call and be forced to sell the stock resulting in additional taxes. This could be a particular problem if the options are ISOs and the margin call results in a disqualifying distribution.

Remember that under Regulation T the maximum that the broker can lend initially is 50% of the market value and only on shares valued over $4 that are publically traded. This loan is called the initial margin. If the stock price drops and the margin loan exceeds 75% of the market value, then the broker must call the loan. You will be required to restore your account to the initial margin amount. If you do not deposit cash or more marginable securities to your account, the broker will sell your stock in order to repay the loan. The broker is not restricted by any company black-out periods or other restrictions on selling the stock.

What is a Reload Feature?

A **reload feature** grants the option holder new (replacement) options when he exercises options by using existing shares of the company's stock to pay for the options. **See Stock Swap.** The reload is tied to the options not the shares. However, you must pay for the new shares with old shares to benefit from the reload. For example, if you use 100 shares currently trading at $100 to exercise 1000 options at $10, you will receive the 1000 shares and the new reload options. The new options will have the same expiry date as the exercised options, but the exercise price will be at the FMV as of the date the new option is issued. Reload features are not very common. Only about 16% of companies use them according to a survey done by the National Association of Stock Plan Professionals (NASPP). There is no tax consequence at the time the reload is granted.

How many new options will I get from a reload?

That depends. Some companies grant one new share for each share that is used to pay for the options. Others will provide one new option for each option that is exercised. A few generous companies will even replace shares that are used to pay the withholding taxes on the exercised options. In some cases, the reload option will also have a reload feature.

Is it possible to have more than one option grant from the same company and to have both ISOs and NQSOs?

Yes. Your company could issue options several times a year. You could receive new option grants every year you are with the company, and you could, over time, receive both ISOs and NQSOs. It is important to keep track of your options, when they will mature, how much the option price is, and any limitations. You will want to develop a game plan for when to exercise which options and keep thorough records of all of your transactions.

The My Records feature of myStockOptions.com is a good place to keep track of basic option information for the do-it-yourselfer, or seek help from your professional advisor.

What happens if I don't or can't exercise my options?

Your options will have a specific life, usually 10 years. If you have not exercised them during that time, your options will expire without value. Since you did not exercise them, you will have no income to recognize and no taxes to pay.

You only want to exercise your options if they are **in-the-money**. In-the-money means that the price of the stock exceeds the price of your option. You certainly would not want to pay $20 for something that is currently only worth $10 regardless of its future potential. In that case, you would let your option expire. However, you do not want to pass up an in-the-money option even if you have to use a cashless option. As noted in Chapter One, however, 11% of in-the-money options expire unexercised.

What happens if I leave my employer before I exercise my options?

When you terminate employment, any non-vested options will be terminated. Your vested options will be exercisable, but usually for only a short time period. According to a survey by the NASPP about 60% of companies allow 90 days following termination to exercise vested options. This is extended for a year for death or disability. Some companies, however, require that the options be exercised before your last day of employment.

ISOs may not be exercised more than three months after termination except for death or disability. If it were allowed by the company, it would be a disqualifying disposition. It is important to check the terms of your options if you have been terminated, are contemplating a new position, or plan on retiring. Make sure you know what your options provide and plan accordingly.

May I exercise my options if my employment is terminated or I quit?

If your employment terminates for any reason, you will be able to exercise any options that are currently vested to you. In most cases, you will have 90 days or less to exercise your vested options. However, some plans may grant longer periods while others may require that you exercise before your last day on the job. The NASPP survey found that 21.5% of plans required options to be exercised before the last day of employment. It is important that you <u>check your plan well before your last day</u>! You will not be able to exercise your non-vested options. In rare cases, where the company is downsizing, it may allow for some non-vested options to be accelerated.

If I become disabled, retire, or die, are there still only 90 days left to exercise?

Not necessarily. Many plans will allow up to a year to exercise vested options in the event of death, disability, or retirement. Again, <u>you must check your plan</u>! The law stipulates that ISOs must be exercised within 90 days of termination to retain ISO treatment. However, the exercise period could be extended to one year for disability and to the expiration date for death. It is up to the employer. In any case, the expiration date is the final date.

How long do I have to exercise my options?

The law requires that ISOs must have an expiration date no later than 10 years from the date of grant. NQSOs could be longer than 10 years. Most companies, however, provide 10 years or less for both ISOs and NQSOs. <u>You must check your company's plan</u>!

Are there any other limits on exercising my options?

Many companies include a non-compete clause in their plans. If you go to work for a competitor, take company secrets, or solicit co-workers to join you at your new company, you may lose your options. Some grants now have a **claw back provision** that requires you to repay the company for any option gains you made in the last six months of employment or more. <u>Check your plan!</u>

My company is going public. How soon after the IPO can I exercise my options?

Assuming your company has granted your options under SEC Rule 701 (a special exemption for pre-IPO company stock), then you will have to wait only 90 days after the IPO. You might be able to sell earlier if your company has filed a Form S-8.

However, the investment banker may require a longer time. This is called the **lock-up** and protects the public from insider trading.

My company pays high dividends. Is that a problem for my stock options?

Dividends are great for stockholders, but not for option holders. *Why?* Dividends are a payout of company earnings and, therefore, tend to depress the company's stock price. Additionally, a dividend payout is money that is not available to reinvest in the business for further growth. Therefore, your options may not have as much potential for increased value. Generally, when the company is paying dividends, you will want to exercise your options as early as possible rather than wait.

Why is it so important to keep thorough records?

Your shares acquired from options are specific in terms of the tax liabilities associated with them. If you have exercised options over a period of time with different option prices, market prices and, therefore, different tax and AMT consequences, you will need to identify which shares you are selling at the time they are sold in order to gain the tax basis associated with those shares. You must direct your broker to sell specific shares! If shares are not specifically identified before the sale, then the FIFO (first in, first out) rules apply. You do not have the average cost convention that you would have when selling mutual fund shares. For example, you have acquired shares with a basis of $10, $20, and $30. Your company stock is now selling at $25. If you direct that the $10 shares be sold, you have a $15 gain. However, you could direct that the $30 shares be sold at a $5 loss. Which is best for your current tax situation? Also, which shares result in long-term and short-term gains or losses?

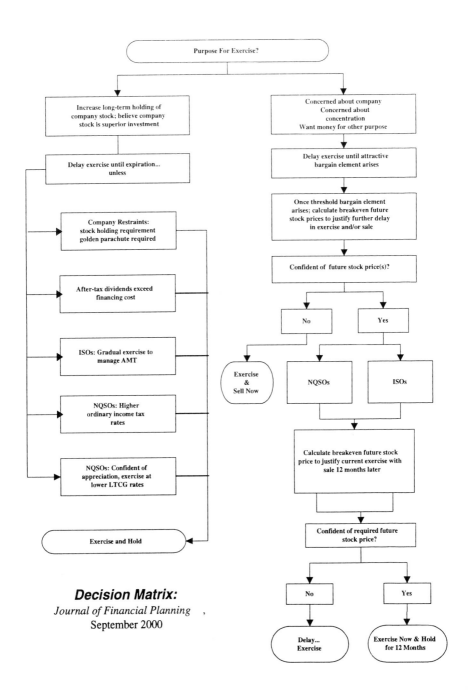

Decision Matrix:

Journal of Financial Planning ,
September 2000

Chapter Eight

What Do I Do With Underwater Options?

What do I do if my options are underwater?

When I wrote the first edition of this book, no one was concerned about their options being worth less (or for that matter worthless) than the option price. Several pages were devoted to the risks of concentrated equity portfolios and the benefits of the Core Capital™ concept (Chapter 14), but few employees were interested. The stock market had sky rocketed through the 90s. Employees had become accustomed to their company's stock increasing 50%, 60% or more every year and prayed that the market would dip just long enough for their new options to be granted. There was no ceiling on how high things could go, or so we thought. Then came the events of 2000/2001. High soaring dot com companies disappeared, technology companies plummeted 80% from their highs, the tragedy of September 11th deepened an already steep economic decline, and then there were the disasters of Enron and Global Crossing. It seemed like there was no bottom.

Surely there will always be times when a company, an industry, or the whole economy will leave employees wondering what to do with their underwater options.

In the worst case, employees who had exercised options and held onto the stock found themselves owing more in taxes than their stock was worth. In one tragic case, an executive, after months of hounding by the IRS for the taxes, simply jumped off a bridge. In Chapter Fourteen, we report on two other stories illustrating the sad results of short sightedness and perhaps greed. There are surely thousands of other examples.

What is an "underwater option"?

An underwater or out-of-the-money option is one in which the option strike price is higher than the current market value of the stock. Therefore, it is currently without market value, but that does not mean that it is without economic value.

How can an underwater option still have value?

Just because your company's stock is currently worth less than the price of your option doesn't mean that it always will be. As employees in the 90s mistakenly came to believe that their company's stock would always be worth more next month, they now believe that it will never be worth more than it is right now. Both are faulty thinking. Let's say that your option was granted in 1999 at $10. Before the market slumped, the price had soared to $30, but now it is only $5. Certainly you would not want to exercise your options now. However, you still have seven years before your option expires. What might your company's stock price hit in the next seven years? Maybe $30, maybe more!

Company will buy underwater options from employees

At least one company, Wright Venture Partners of New York, offers employers a plan whereby Wright will buy options from the employees at a discounted price. Wright is providing liquidity to employees who may have thought that their options were worthless. At the same time, Wright plans to make a significant profit when many of the companies return to respectable market values well above the discounted price Wright is paying.

My company is going to reprice my options. What does that mean?

Not that long ago, it meant that the company simply canceled out your old options and issued you new ones at the current price. There was no tax consequence to you or the company. Many people thought this was a bad practice. Options were meant to provide an incentive to grow the company, but if the market price didn't go up, only the shareholders bore the risk. The employee option holders were protected from market risk at the shareholders expense.

FASB Interpretation No. 44, *Accounting for Certain Transactions Involving Stock Compensation*, adopted in July 2000, changed that. Now if a company reprices options, it must account for the new options as variable options. That means that rather than no charge to earnings, the company must take a compensation expense charge to earnings for any increase in the price of the shares at the time the executive exercised his options. This is a tremendous unknown future expense to the corporation. As a result, many companies are no longer repricing options.

**Can't my company just issue me new options at the current
market price?**

Your company could issue new shares, but what do you do
with the old shares. If you just keep the old shares, the
shareholders could see a substantial diiution of their interest at a
later date. If you have 1000 options now at $25 and the company
issues you 1000 new options at $20 (the current market price); you
may end up exercising both sets of options as the company's stock
price climbs in the future.

Alternatively, your company could have you surrender your
existing options for the issue of new options. However, to avoid
the tax consequences of FASB No. 44, the company will not be
able to issue your replacement options until six months and a day
later. In some cases, the company will provide fewer replacement
options than those surrendered.

**Does it make sense to turn my options in for new options six
months later?**

Maybe, maybe not. You know what you have now; but you
have no way of knowing what things will be like six months and a
day from now. What if the price of the stock jumps? Your new
options could be much higher than your old ones? What if you
terminate employment? Options are not for former employees.
Unless you are substantially underwater, you may be better off
holding the ones you have.

From the shareholder's prospective, there is a danger to this
approach as well. The employee, this would include senior
management with lots of options, actually has an interest in
keeping the stock price down during this time period.

What about replacing my options with restricted stock?

A few companies are doing this. The employee exchanges his options for restricted stock. The stock vests over a period of years, thus acting as a retention tool and the company gets to write off the expense over four years. Of course, you are converting your options to shares at a price below your option price. It seems like it would be better to buy shares in the open market without restrictions.

Couldn't the company just accelerate my future options?

This is being done in some cases. However, many shareholders are objecting to the practice since they believe that management (and other employees) are being protected from the market and rewarded for poor performance. Some things the company might do: 1) if you normally get your option grant in December, it could be moved up to March; 2) if you get 1000 options per year, you might get 250 options per quarter. The result is the same, just the timing changes thus not causing an undue burden for the shareholders.

Can I exchange my options for a nonqualified deferred compensation plan with the company?

According to PLR 199901006, an executive who turns his options in for a nonqualified deferred compensation plan with his employer will incur no income tax consequences until the benefits are paid out. Of course, a nonqualified deferred compensation plan is a unsecured promise by the corporation to pay benefits to the executive in the future. Should the company fail, the executive must stand in line with all of the other creditors.

I have vested grants that are in-the-money and ones that are underwater. Can't I exercise both and offset the losses against the gains?

No. The spread for the in-the-money options is ordinary income and subject to payroll taxes as well as income tax. The sale of stock from the underwater options results in a short-term capital loss, giving you only a partial benefit against the taxes you incurred on the in-the-money options. It makes no sense to pay more for something using your options than you would pay in the open market. Besides, if your options still have years to go before maturity, they might well be worth more in the future.

I exercised my ISOs and incurred the AMT. Now my stock options are much lower than my exercise price, what can I do?

If you are in the same tax year, you should sell your shares before year-end. This will result in a disqualifying disposition and eliminate the AMT. If the tax year has closed, you now have an AMT credit that will carry forward. It may take many years before you fully benefit from your AMT credit. If your company's stock regains its value, you will find the AMT credit beneficial in reducing your taxes upon sale. See Chapter Six and discuss with your tax advisor transactions that will allow you to use your AMT credit.

Underwater Option Alternatives

Approach	Leave options intact and accelerate next grant	Replace options with restricted stock	Cancel and replace the options six months plus a day later
Description	Company makes new grants or accelerate grants	Company replaces options with restricted stock	Company cancels option and issues new ones six months plus a day later
Company's accounting expense	None	Recognize fixed cost equal to grant value	None, but this is an issue that is being debated
Risks	Results in a wind fall to the ee if stock rebounds, unfair to shareholders	Shares have restrictions on them. May get fewer shares than options	Market risk if share price rises, out of the market for six months, may leave company
Best used	Company has sufficient shares in the option plan to make additional grants	Company wants to make sure employees remain tied to the stock	Options are so deeply underwater, that ee's consider them worthless

Approach	Trade options for non-qualified deferred comp.	Buy out options with cash	Sell options to a third party
Description	Company provides you with a deferred comp. agreement in exchange for your shares	Company buys out your options based on a discount formula	You sell your options to a third party at a negotiated price
Company's accounting expense	None	Recognize fixed cost for cash payment	None if options are vested
Risks	Un-secured creditor of company, must wait till deferral date, don't participate in equity growth	Possible variable accounting (FASB 44), no chance for future recovery of stock	Company has new class of non-employee option holders
Best used	Employee wants certainty of value and believes company is not at risk	Company has cash and can absorb the accounting cost	Company has other incentives for ee, and is OK with outside option holders

Copyright Wheeler/Frost Associates, Inc. 2002

Chapter Nine

May I Gift My Stock Options?

Can my options be gifted to avoid estate taxes?

If the options are transferrable (ISOs are never transferable), you can gift the options to your children, a trust, or charity. The value of the options will not be included in your estate if the gift is a completed gift (Private Letter Rulings 9725032 and 9722022).

If I make a gift of my options, am I subject to gift taxes?

Yes. You may take advantage of the $10,000 per year annual exclusion and your lifetime exemption to avoid taxes. If you and your spouse have three children, you could give them $60,000 in options in one year ($10,000 per spouse, per child). Each of you could also use your lifetime exemption of $700,000 for 2002 and 2003. The exemption will climb to $1,000,000 per person in 2006.

How is the value of the gift determined?

A stock option has value by virtue of the holder's ability to take advantage of the appreciation potential of the stock without committing his or her own resources or taking any of the risks associated with ownership. However, there is no legal or administrative precedent for determining the value of stock options for gift tax purposes. The IRS has announced that the gift tax regulations should be used in valuing stock options. The value of the gift of the option would be measured by the **willing buyer/willing seller test**. The gift could be less than the spread used for determining your tax liability on the exercise of the options since the value would be determined as of the date of your gift and reflective of the volatility of the stock and other factors that could result in a discount to the spread.

Willing buyer/willing seller seems a little vague. Is there a way to be sure of the value for gift tax purposes?

The prevailing model for determining the value of executive stock options for more than 20 years has been the **Black-Scholes model**. This model is based on the premise that a stock option has value by virtue of the holder's ability to take advantage of the appreciation potential of the underlying stock without committing his or her own resources or taking any of the risks associated with stock ownership. Black-Scholes factors in the stock's volatility, the current risk-free interest rate, the option's strike price, the stock's current market value, and the dividend rate on the stock. From this price you may be able to take a discount for lack of marketability and vesting restrictions. **See Black-Scholes Formula.**

Neither the IRS nor any courts (as of this writing) have required the use of the Black-Scholes model for determining the value of gifted options.

Until they do, we would suggest you use the IRS estate tax ruling for valuing gifted options; that is the intrinsic value as measured by the FMV minus the exercise price (the spread). Whether you use Black-Scholes, willing buyer/willing seller, or the intrinsic value; if your gift is substantial, you should have a professional set the value of the gifted options for you. At some point, the IRS will look for that independent valuation.

Black-Scholes Formula

For those of you who want to attempt to use the Black-Scholes formula, I have included it. As you can see, it is very complex.

$$C = SN(\ln(S/K) + (r+o^2/2)^t)/(o\sqrt{t})) - K(e)^{(-rt)} N((\ln(S/K) + (r+o^2/2)^t)/(o\sqrt{t})) - o\sqrt{t}$$

The explanation of the variables in the Black-Scholes formula are:

N = cumulative standard normal distribution
C = theoretical call premium   **S** = current stock price
t = time until option expiration   **K** = option stock price
r = risk free interest rate   **ln** = natural logarithm
e = exponential function   **o** = standard deviation of stock returns

---

Do I still need an appraisal, if my gift is more modest?

As noted above, neither the IRS nor the courts have ruled that any one valuation method is required. For now, you may rely on the IRS's estate tax ruling that measures the option's value by reference to its intrinsic value (the spread). Rev. Proc 98-34 contains guidance on valuing non-publically traded stock.

Am I subject to income on the options if I make a gift of them?

No. IRC Section 83 does not require you to recognize income for compensation purposes until the value of the income is readily determinable. Until the options are exercised, their value cannot be determined. You have reduced your taxable estate without having to pay the income tax.

When the options are exercised, who recognizes the income?

Only the employee is subject to income taxes. (IRC Section 83), the beneficiaries have merely received the options as a gift. They did not perform services for the employer. When the recipient exercises the options, the employee or donor will have to pay all the payroll taxes. The good news is that this is a further reduction in your taxable estate.

Is there a risk that my children may exercise the options when I don't want them to?

Yes, there is that risk. Once you have gifted the options, you no longer have control over their execution. You may want to consider using a trust rather than an outright gift so you can have some control over the timing of the exercise for tax purposes.

If my stock options are subject to acceleration when I terminate my employment, may I still gift it?

In PLR 9616035, the IRS ruled that an option subject to acceleration could still be gifted. The IRS observed that ". . . these are acts of independent significance and any effect such termination may have on the exercise of the options is only collateral or incidental to termination of employment." In other words, no problem.

What happens if I die before my options are exercised?

There is some uncertainty as to who is responsible for the Section 83 (employment) income should your options be exercised after your death. PLR 9616035 provides that if the taxpayer (that's you) is not alive when the options are exercised, then the estate will be deemed to have received the Section 83 compensation. However, Regulation 1.83-1(d) indicates that the property would be treated as **income in respect of a decedent** (IRD).

A question to consider: *if your options are exercised several years after your death and your estate has been closed, who pays the taxes?* If possible, the options should be exercised before your death. This will avoid any question as to how they might be taxed. Additionally, the income tax paid will not be included in your estate. Since we can't always plan for our deaths, the second best approach would be for the estate to exercise the options before the final distribution of the estate assets and for the executor to determine what assets will be used to pay the taxes.

Can I gift the options to a trust?

Yes. In place of outright gifts, you could make a gift to a trust. In Private Letter Rulings 9725032 and 9722022, the IRS determined that the transfer of options to a trust was a completed gift, and neither the options nor the stock obtained by exercise was included in the optionee's gross estate.

Are there any income tax advantages to a gift in trust?

Under sub-chapter J, grantor trust, if the grantor retains certain powers, the income, deductions, and credits of the trust are treated as items of income, deduction, and credit of the grantor, not the trust. There are four powers that cause the trust gift to be incomplete for income tax purposes, but complete for estate and gift tax purposes. The powers are:

1. The right, held by the grantor, to reacquire trust property by substitution.
2. The power, held by a non-adverse party, but not the grantor, to control the beneficial enjoyment by the beneficiaries of the trust property.
3. The power to borrow from the trust without adequate security.
4. Actually borrowing from the trust.

The power to control beneficial enjoyment would include adding to the beneficiaries named. This power may be held by the spouse of the grantor. The grantor trust is an effective tool for transferring more to the beneficiaries since the payment of the taxes under Section 83 at the time of option exercise and the subsequent capital gains tax on sale of the stock are not additional gifts to the beneficiaries. The donor has, thereby, reduced his estate by the gift and all of the taxes on it. (PLR 9543049)

Can I make a gift to a charity of my stock options?
You cannot gift ISOs, however, you could gift NQSOs to a charity. Since, under Section 83, the exercise of options is taxable to the employee, it is questionable as to the benefit one would receive by making such a gift.

When making a charitable gift of options, you would be entitled to an immediate tax deduction equal to the current fair market value of the option. Based on Black-Scholes, this could be as little as 30% of the actual market price of the stock. For example, you have options to buy your company's stock at $10 and it is currently trading at $50. You would be able to claim a charitable deduction for $15. Assume the charity holds the options for six months and exercises at $80. Remember, under IRC Section 83, you are responsible for the payroll taxes. You end up paying taxes on $70 (the spread) which are greater than the tax benefit you gained on the gift. Therefore, generally, you will be better off to exercise the option and gift the stock.

Are there any ways to make the option gift and control the tax consequences?

In the case sited in PLR 9737016, the client retained the right to veto the charity's exercise of the donated options. The IRS stated that the gift was not complete until the charity exercised. While the executive didn't get a current deduction, he did get the benefit of making the gift to the charity currently and got the full benefit of the gift at the time when it would best serve his needs.

In PLR 9737015, the taxpayer deposited options into an escrow account with his bank. Under the terms of the escrow, the taxpayer couldn't take back the options but he could direct when they would be exercised and which charities would benefit. The IRS stated that the gift was not complete and that the taxpayer would get his deduction at the time of exercise.

What are Entrepreneurs' Foundations?

Entrepreneurs' Foundations are charitable foundations that have focused on start-up companies for donations of pre-IPO stock options. By attracting smaller companies before they become public, entrepreneurs' foundations hope to participate in the next big stock market win. The advantage of these foundations over other charities is that they are specifically looking for the pre-IPO option. Many older charities may not be willing to accept shares or options from start-up companies. The issues discussed above still apply to charitable giving.

If I decide I want to make a gift of my options, how do I go about it?

Review your options to make sure that they are transferable. Determine the value of the options using an appropriate valuation method to determine the taxable gift, if any. Transfer the stock options to the donee using the appropriate legal documents. When the stock options are exercised, include the income (spread) with your taxable income and be sure to have the appropriate taxes withheld.

When the stock is sold, if it's held by a sub-chapter J grantor trust, you will recognize the taxable gain or loss. If it is not held by a grantor trust, the donee will recognize the capital gain or loss based on your cost basis.

Are there any risks in giving my options away?

Yes. You could have a liquidity problem when the options are exercised and you have to pay the taxes. The IRS could change its position on the gifting of options and treat the income taxes paid as additional gifts. The value of the stock could decrease after the gift causing a waste of the gift tax or exemption you used in making the gift.

Chapter Ten

How Do Stock Options Fit Into My Estate Plan?

If I die while holding stock options, are they included in my estate?

Yes. If the option holder dies while holding options that are exercisable after his death, then the value of the options are includable in his estate. In most cases, this would be your vested options. The value of the options at the date of death includes all appreciation that occurred between the date of grant and the date of death. The IRS has ruled that the estate value is the difference between the option price (strike price) and the market price, in other words, the spread. The spread is also considered income in respect of decedent (IRD).

IRC Section 2032 provides that the executor may select the date of death or the alternate valuation date six months hence to value the estate assets. This would include your options.

Will my estate be subject to FICA and Medicare taxes?

No. The exercise will constitute ordinary income, but will not be reported on a W-2 subject to payroll taxes.

Who pays the taxes on options exercised after my death?

The answer to this is not clear. PLR 9616035 provides that if the taxpayer is not living when the options are exercised, then the taxpayer's estate will be deemed to have received the Section 83 compensation. However, IRS Regulation 1.83-1(d) indicates that if the property is still substantially non-vested when the donor dies, then Section 691 will apply. Section 691 provides that only income that is not recognized by the decedent before death will be recognized by the recipient when the donor dies. The only safe bet here, if you know you are dying, is to have your trust or the recipient of your options exercise the options so that you will incur the taxes prior to your death.

Either the estate or the option beneficiary, depending on which one exercises the options, will have to pay the taxes. However, IRC Section 691(c) provides that the taxpayer subject to the IRD is entitled to a deduction for the estate tax attributable to the value of the options included in the estate.

Can the options be gifted to avoid the estate taxes?

If the options are transferrable, you can gift the options to your children, to a trust, or to a family limited partnership. The value of the options will not be included in your estate if the gift is a completed gift. (Private Letter Rulings 9725032 and 9722022) **See Chapter Nine.**

What about my ISOs?

ISOs cannot be gifted or transferred to anyone, including a trust (Regulation Section 1.421-7(b)-2). However, at death, ISOs can be transferred by a will, by laws of descent, or by a beneficiary designation including to a trust.

Are there any other considerations for ISOs?

Yes. When heirs exercise ISOs, there are no payroll taxes due and the stock gets a "step-up" in basis to the fair market value at death. However, the AMT still applies.

What if my options are underwater at my death?

If your options are underwater (having a market value below your option price), then there would be no value to include in your estate. Remember that the intrinsic value for estate tax purposes is the spread. If the options subsequently are in-the-money before they expire, then your estate could realize a gain without having an estate tax liability. On NQSOs, your estate would still have Section 83 income, Income in Respect of a Decedent (IRD). **See Chapter Nine.**

Is there a way to retain the income tax consequences while making a completed gift for estate tax purposes?

A grantor trust, under sub-chapter J allows the grantor to obtain all tax consequences (income and deductions) of the trust. To qualify as a grantor trust, the grantor must retain certain powers over the trust. These include: the right of the grantor to reacquire trust property by substitution; the power held by a non-adverse party to control the beneficial enjoyment by beneficiaries; the power to borrow from the trust without adequate security; and actually borrowing from the trust. **See Chapter Nine.**

What would be the reason to retain the income tax consequences?

By retaining the income tax consequences, you will pay both the Section 83 income taxes on the exercise (required) and the capital gains taxes on the sale of the stock. Your estate will be reduced by the amount of the taxes as well as the gift.

Clearly, the Section 83 income belongs to the donor and is not subject to gift taxes. The capital gains tax under a sub-chapter J grantor trust is less clear. In PLR 9444033, the IRS found that such an arrangement did constitute an additional gift. However, in PLR 9543049, the IRS reversed its position without further explanation or comment.

What happens if I die before the options are exercised?

To repeat what was said earlier, there is some uncertainty as to who is responsible for the Section 83 employment income should your options be exercised after your death. As noted previously, PLR 9616035 provides that if the taxpayer is not alive when the options are exercised, then his/her estate will be deemed to have received the Section 83 compensation. However, Regulation 1.83-1(d) indicates that the property would be treated as IRD and the tax paid by the person who exercises the options.

If my options are exercised several years after my death and my estate has been closed, who pays the taxes?

If possible, the options should be exercised before your death. This will avoid any question as to how they might be taxed, since there is no clear answer to this question. Additionally, the income tax paid will not be included in your estate. As to the question, it is not clear who will pay the taxes. Most likely, they will be paid by the person who exercises the options.

Can I make a Testamentary gift to Charity of my NQSOs?

Yes. The income on exercise would be IRD, taxable to the charity (which is not taxed) not to the donor's estate. Additionally, the estate is entitled to an estate tax charitable deduction.

As the executor/trustee do I have any risk in holding options in the estate/trust?

Yes. You must immediately determine the option expiration dates for the options in the estate or trust. In many cases, the expiration date is accelerated at death. If you don't exercise, in time you could be personally liable to the heirs for the loss. Should you delay exercise or exercise right away is another issue. The estate may not have the assets to exercise the options. You will need to make sure that you have the power to borrow (margin) and to sell assets in case a cashless exercise is required. These are not easy discussions for the executor/trustee and each discussion is faced with the risk of being second guessed by disgruntled heirs in the future.

Steps to Take When Transferring Options for Estate Planning Purposes

1. Check that your options are transferable - does your plan allow you to transfer your shares to family, a trust, FLP, charity?
2. Who should receive the options - children, grandchildren?
3. Does a trust or family limited partnership make sense?
4. Run the numbers using different assumptions - get help from someone with stock option expertise and software capable of testing various assumptions.
5. Determine the value of the options for gift purposes - you will need to know the value of the gift for gift tax purposes.
6. Understand the financial downrides - if the value of the options goes down, you will loose the gift taxes you have paid.
7. Transfer vested options first - a gift is not complete until the options are vested.
8. Plan for your income tax liability when the options are exercised - remember under Section 83(b) you remain liable for the tax on the spread.
9. Consider the ramifications of the transfer - transferred options still count as yours for proxy compensation purposes.
10. Remember Section 16 rules - gifts need to be reported.

Based on: *Save on Estate Taxes with Transferable Stock Options*, Susan Daley, myStockOptions.com

Chapter Eleven

What Happens to My Options If I Get Divorced?

The impact of divorce goes far beyond the economic issues addressed in this chapter. However, since so many marriages now result in a divorce and more than 60% of all second (or more) marriages do not last, we must address this issue. Unfortunately, there is not a lot of legal precedent to go on.

With the explosion of stock option grants, the value of stock options, in many cases, will be the major asset of the marital estate. Family law courts have had trouble understanding some of the more common assets such as pension plans and the application of a Qualified Domestic Relations Order (QUDRO) in a divorce situation. Now they are struggling to deal with the complexities of stock options and the uniqueness of each option agreement.

What is Community Property?

Community property consists of assets that are earned during marriage in community property states (Arizona, California,

Idaho, Louisiana, Nevada, New Mexico, Texas, Washington, and Wisconsin) from your labor, investments, etc. It does not include gifts, inheritance, assets that were acquired prior to marriage if maintained as separate property, and personal injury awards. A stock option is granted as part of a compensation plan, therefore, it is included in community property.

What is Separate Property?

Separate property consists of assets that are acquired prior to marriage, by gift, inheritance, and earnings in the 41 separate property states. Even though the fruits of your earnings may be separate property, many states will still split the assets similar to community property in a divorce.

How are stock options treated in a divorce?

This depends on a lot of factors and there is no guarantee that your situation will be treated the same as someone else's or that the court will come to the same conclusion as in other cases.

In four California cases, the courts found that options owned, exercised, and fully vested before the date of separation were community property and a part of the marital estate.

In cases where the options were granted during the marriage, but could only be exercised after the separation, the courts found that the non-employee spouse had only a partial interest depending on timing. In *Marriage of Hug (1984) 154 Cal. App. 3d 780, Marriage of Nelson (1986) 177 Cal. App. 3d 150*, and *Marriage of Harrison (1986) 179 Cal. App. 3d 1216*, the California courts established the **time rule**. Under this approach, the courts granted the non-option holding spouse with a fractional interest. Many other courts have followed California's lead. **See Example 11.1.**

Example 11.1

Time Rule =

time (months) from beginning of spouse's
employment to date of separation

---

time (months) from beginning of spouse's
employment to date option can be exercised

Can options be used to determine child support?

Yes. The income recognized from the exercise of options could be included in your income for determining child support payments.

How do you determine the value of stock options for divorce purposes?

It seems reasonable that the value would be the spread as it is for tax purposes. However, the question then is: the spread as of when? Is it as of the date of separation, the date of vesting (when the option can first be exercised), or the date of actual exercise (which could be several years after the divorce).

The *Went* case in Connecticut approached this issue using the time rule, then went on to consider the following in determining the value of the spouse's interest:

Factors include, but certainly are not limited to:

1) when the option was granted;
2) whether the option was granted for past or future performance;
3) whether or not the option was granted in lieu of other compensation;
4) whether or not the option was an incentive stock option or nonqualified stock option;

5) when the option will expire;

6) the tax effect on the exercise;

7) whether or not the option has a reasonably ascertainable fair market value;

8) whether or not the option is transferable;

9) whether or not the option is restricted;

10) the extent to which the option is subject to forfeiture;

11) any other factors that could affect the value.

Interestingly, the court rejected the wife's expert valuation using the Black-Scholes model and instead opted for the intrinsic value approach.

The value for determining the material estate allocation may not be the same as it is for income tax purposes. The court will determine the method it uses to allocate the estate. The IRS will decide how you will be taxed on the results. Rev. Proc. 98-34 contains guidance on valuing non-publicly traded stock. Non-publicly traded stock may be much more difficult and more expensive to value.

When and how does the non-option spouse receive his/her interest?

We know that only an employee can hold an ISO and that NQSOs can be transferred to others without consequences. However, the employee remains liable for the Section 83 income taxes.

How then will the court grant an interest in the options to the non-option spouse? Does the non-option spouse simply have a future interest in the employee spouse's exercise? Will the non-option spouse have to wait for the employee spouse's decision to exercise? Can the non-option spouse force the employee spouse to exercise at the first opportunity? If the non-option spouse receives NQSOs and then exercises, how does the employee spouse get reimbursed for the payroll taxes?

The courts have come up with two approaches, the **deferred distribution method** and the **present value with offset against the other assets method**.

In *Callahan vs. Callahan (New Jersey)*, the court ruled that the options acquired by the husband were subject to equitable distribution even though they would not vest until after the divorce. The court impressed a constructive trust on the husband in favor of the wife in order to best affect the distribution of the option proceeds once exercised.

In the present value method, the courts have fashioned various approaches to transfer interest to the spouse. The cleanest approach is to transfer options to the spouse when the options can be transferred. Some courts have required the parties to hold the options as tenants-in-common.

Another approach is to determine the present value of the options and give the spouse other assets from the estate to offset the value of the options retained by the other spouse. Of course, this carries substantial risk for both parties. If the stock goes down in value, the options may not be exercised, or the employed spouse may quit or lose his or her job and not vest. Alternatively, the stock may skyrocket after the divorce.

Are stock options subject to a Qualified Domestic Relations Order (QUDRO)?

No. A QUDRO is the legal device that allows for the division of an employee's qualified retirement plan (pension, profit sharing, 401K) in a divorce. It does not apply to a stock option plan.

What happens if I transfer ISOs as a result of my divorce?

As noted earlier, the IRS has held that the transfer of an ISO converts it to an NQSO. IRC Sec. 422(b)(5) provides that an ISO cannot be transferrable by the employee except at death and that an ISO must be ". . . exercisable, during his lifetime, only by the [employee]." IRC Sec. 422(c)(4)(A) provides that an inter-spousal transfer incident to divorce under Sec. 1041(a) are ". . . not treated as a disposition." Sec 424(c)(4)(B) provides that the tax treatment ". . . shall apply to the transferee as it would have applied to the transferor."

This may lead one to incorrectly assume that an ISO or NQSO could be transferred without consequence. Not so. Section 424(c)(4)(A) would only apply if the employee had already exercised the options and held the stock. Sec. 424(c)(4)(B) applies only at death not divorce.

What do I do if the court directs that I give my spouse half of my ISOs?

First, of course, the court needs to understand the tax consequences of the event and approve a tax efficient approach. Given that, there are two options:

1. If you are vested, exercise the options and given you ex-spouse his/her share of the stock. If the court approves, this should be net of the current tax consequences.
2. If you are not vested or there could be a better time to exercise, enter into an agreement whereby you agree to transfer shares as the options are exercised.

Is there a different tax treatment if my options are community property?

While options may be community property under state law, IRC Sec. 422(b)(5) provides that only the employee can exercise ISOs. Therefore, the transfer of ISOs to a spouse will result in the options being disqualified.

A community property split of NQSOs does not result in a tax consequence (absent exercise). There is no recognition of income under IRC Sec. 83. (PLR 9433010) On exercise each spouse will be subject to income taxes, but the employed spouse will be responsible for the payroll taxes.

What if I pay my spouse for his/her community interest in my stock options with other assets?

The IRS has concluded in PLR 8813023 and Field Service Advice (FSA) 20005006 that this is essentially a deemed sale, and, therefore, the spouse is taxed on the cash payments. The taxpayer appealed the findings of PLR 8813023 to the tax court and won. In *Balding v. Commissioner,* 98 TC 368 (1992), the court agreed with the taxpayer that Sec. 1041 protected her from gain recognition and rejected the IRS's position.

However, in FSA 20005006 the IRS ignored the *Balding* case since it involved a deferred compensation plan which the IRS now agrees is subject to Sec. 1041. The IRS views the transfer of stock options as akin to the transfer of service income not property and, therefore, not covered by Sec. 1041.

What are the tax consequences if I transfer options subject to a divorce decree?

IRC Section 1041 provides that gain is not recognized when property is transferred between spouse or former spouses incident to a divorce. However, in FSA 20005006, the IRS rejected Sec. 1041 and concluded that an employee who transfers stock options to a spouse or former spouse subject to a divorce must recognize income immediately even though the option has not been exercised.

The FSA noted that upon transfer, the ISOs became NQSOs. This makes sense since ISOs are non-transferrable. However, the IRS went on to the state that the transfer was a taxable arm's-length disposition of the options under Sec. 1.83-1 (b)(1) resulting in compensation income to the employee spouse as of the date of transfer. The IRS's position is that Sec. 1041 does not encompass compensation income to the employee spouse as of the date of transfer. The FSA is consistent with Temporary Regulation Sec. 1.1041-1T A-4 which declares that ". . . transfers of services are not subject to the rules of Section 1041."

The good news is there would not be another taxable event when the ex-spouse does exercise the options.

Chapter Twelve

What If I Am an Affiliate or Insider?

What is an affiliated person?

If you are an insider, officer, or holder of 10% or more of the company's stock, you are probably an **affiliated person** under the terms of the Securities Act of 1933, Rule 144. An insider is a person who has executive policy making responsibility and access to confidential company information. If you meet any of these definitions, your stock will be restricted.

What is Rule 144?

Rule 144 is designed to implement the fundamental purposes of the Securities Act of 1933, as expressed in its preamble, "To provide full and fair disclosure of the character of the securities sold in interstate commerce and through the mail, and to prevent fraud in the sale thereof . . . "

The purpose and underlying policy of the Act require that there be adequate current information concerning the issuer.

Accordingly, the availability of the rule is conditioned on the existence of adequate current public information.

A holding period prior to the resale of the shares is essential to assure that controlling persons have assumed the economic risks of investment, and, therefore, are not acting as conduits for sale to the public of unregistered securities, directly or indirectly, on behalf of an issuer.

Definitions:

Affiliate of an issuer - a person who directly or indirectly, through one or more intermediaries, controls, or is controlled by, or is under common control with such issuer.

Person - the person for whose account securities are to be sold including all of the following persons: any relative or spouse of such person, or any relative of such spouse; anyone who has the same home as such person; any trust or estate in which such person or any of the persons specified collectively own 10% or more of the total beneficial interest; any corporation or other organization (other than the issuer) in which such person is a beneficial owner of 10% or more of any class of equity securities or 10% or more of the equity interest.

Restricted securities - securities acquired directly or indirectly from the issuer, or from an affiliate of the issuer, in a transaction or chain of transactions not involving any public offering; securities acquired from the issuer that are subject to the resale limitations of Rule 502(d) under Regulation D or Rule 701(c); securities acquired in a transaction or chain of transactions meeting the requirements of Rule 144A; securities acquired from the issuer in a transaction subject to the conditions of Regulation CE; equity securities of domestic issuers acquired in a transaction or chain of transactions subject to the conditions of Rule 901 or Rule 903 under Regulation S; securities acquired in a transaction made under Rule 801 to the same extent and proportion that the securities held by the security holder of the class with respect to which the rights offering was made, were, as of the record date for the rights offering, "restricted securities" within the meaning of this paragraph (a)(3); and securities acquired in a transaction made under Rule 802 to the same extent and proportion that the securities that were tendered or exchanged in the exchange offer or business combination were "restricted securities" within the meaning of this paragraph (a)(3).

As you can see, this is not an area to go it alone. If you are or might be considered an affiliate or controlling person, get professional advice.

What is the holding period for restricted securities?

If you sell restricted securities you must have held the securities for a minimum of one year between the later of the date of 1) your acquisition of the securities from the issuer or 2) from an affiliate of the issuer, and any resale of such securities. The one-year period doesn't begin until the purchase price or other consideration is paid in full.

How does an affiliated person sell his stock?

There are five requirements an affiliated person must meet to sell stock under Rule 144:

1) Adequate public information must be available about the company.
2) The volume limitations of Rule 144 must be met.

3) The sale must be made by an NASD licensed broker.
4) A Form 144 must be filed.
5) If the securities are "restricted" they can not be sold until one year after the date of purchase.

How soon after an IPO can I sell my stock under Rule 144?

You must wait at least 90 days. Additionally, the underwriter may impose a longer "lock-up period."

What are the volume limitations of Rule 144?

The amount of stock being sold by an affiliate, along with all other sales by the affiliate in the prior three months, cannot exceed the greater of: 1) 1% of the outstanding common stock of the company; or 2) the average weekly reported volume of trading in the company's stock during the four calender weeks before the filing of Form 144.

Are there any other restrictions on my stock options?

Yes. The Securities Exchange Act of 1934, Section 16(b), provides that a corporation can recover from an insider any profits made from short-term trading. This means trades within six months. However, Rule 16(b)(3) allows options to be transferable so long as they are a gift to a family member or family trust. Of course, this would only apply to NQSOs since ISOs are non-transferable.

Who is subject to Section 16?

Section 16 covers every person who is a director, executive officer, or owner of 10% or more of a public company. The term officer includes the president, the principal financial officer, principal accounting officer, vice presidents in charge of business units, any officer who preforms a significant policy-making function, and any other person who performs similar policy-making functions. These persons must report their trades and other financial disclosures on Forms 3, 4, and 5.

What are Forms 3, 4, and 5?

Form 3 is the initial report. It must be filed within 10 days after a director or officer assumes office and shows how much company stock he holds.

Form 4 reports changes in stock ownership and must be filed soon after the event. Form 4 would be filed for a purchase, sale, exercise of options, gift, transfer to a trust, etc..

Form 5 is filed before the 45th day following the close of the corporate fiscal year. It reports all transactions that were not previously reported on Form 4 during the year.

What are short-swing profits under Section 16?

To prevent insiders from speculating in company stock, Section 16 aggregates all of the purchases and sales by an affiliate in the last six months. Any "short-swing profits" from such activity are returned to the company. It doesn't matter what your motivation was for the trades.

Do Rule 144 and Section 16 apply to my gifting of stock?

Yes. If you gift your stock, the donee is subject to Rule 144 the same as you are.

Gifts to family members, however, are exempt from Section 16 reporting.

As an affiliate person can I participate in the ESPP?

If the ESPP is a qualified plan under Section 423, you will be alright. There is no Section 16 reporting for electing to participate. The purchase of shares through the ESPP is exempt from the short-swing profits liability. However, a sale of ESPP shares is subject to the short-swing profits liability. Additionally, you must report your holdings (not the purchase) and the sales on Form 4.

May I gift my shares to family members?

Subject to your plan, yes. **See Chapter Ten**. However, you and your family remain subject to Rule 144 and Section 16.

May I donate my shares to charity and then buy back the shares through exercise of an option or open market purchase?

Yes. The wash sale rule does not apply to a charitable gift. Additionally, the gift is not subject to Section 16(b) "short-swing profits liability."

Since I am restricted from selling my shares, am I entitled to a discount for tax purposes?

Probably not. To discount the stock's value from its market price at the exercise date, the stock must be subject to a restriction that never lapses. Rule 144 requires insiders to hold stock for one year from the date of acquisition. Section 16(b) attempts to prevent speculation on "short-swings" and looks at the last six months. Thus any diminution to the stock's FMV at exercise is short-term and cannot be used for establishing a discount.

However, to delay a taxable event, the stock must only be subject to a substantial risk of forfeiture and nontransferable. Section 83(c)(3) provides that, as long as the sale of property could subject a person to suit under Section 16(b) then the person's rights to the property are both subject to a substantial risk of forfeiture and are nontransferable. Thus, you may be able to defer taxes on your option exercise for six months or longer. This could help with some tax planning.

Be sure to work with your employer on this. If your employer issues you a W-2 including your option compensation, then you are deemed to have received the income in that year regardless of any risk of forfeiture.

What about a blockage discount?

If you are a non-affiliated employee of a company that has a large volume of stock traded, it is unlikely that you could qualify for a discount. However, if you have a large quantity of options that you are exercising and the average monthly sales volume of your company's stock is not very high, you might qualify for a **blockage discount.** If the facts are right, it is worth checking.

With restrictions and lock-ups, it seems like there is never a time that I can sell my stock. Is there some way to systematically reduce my exposure?

Yes. In Security and Exchange Commission Regulation FD (Full Disclosure), the SEC published Rule 10b5-1 which allows insiders to establish plans for the future trades of their company stock. <u>The plan must be established when the executive doesn't have any knowledge of non-public information that could materially effect the company's prospects</u>. The executive can develop any reasonable plan such as selling 1000 shares per month, selling 5000 shares on the first trading day of each quarter, or exercise options and sell the shares one month before each date on which college tuition is due.

By following Rule 10b5-1, the executive has an affirmative defense against any insider trading charges. To implement the plan you need to have your corporate legal council check to make sure that you comply with the company's insider trading policies.

Chapter Thirteen

I Have Substantial Option Value. Are There Any Advanced Planning Concepts?

The issues of exercise, taxation, concentrated exposure, estate planning, etc. discussed in this book are the same for an employee with a few thousand shares or an executive with several million. However, there are issues that are unique to the highly compensated executive. Many of those were discussed in the prior chapter dealing with an affiliated person. This chapter covers a variety of planning techniques that may benefit you if your options represent a substantial amount of potential wealth. Be sure to read about concentrated risk in Chapter Fourteen.

What are my choices if I have a highly concentrated portfolio due to my options and holdings of company stock?

You have a few choices:

1. Hold the stock and hope that it continues to climb or at least not decline. (Not the best idea.)

2. Sell the stock or exercise and sell the options subject to ordinary income and payroll taxes, AMT, and short or long term capital gains.
3. Enter into one of several hedging strategies, so that you don't currently incur the taxes while mitigating your concentrated market risk.

What is a hedging strategy?

Hedging is used to reduce or eliminate the price volatility of the stock. The simplest hedge would be the purchase of a put. The put would give you the right to sell your stock at a given price. Then when your option vests, your stock is eligible for long-term capital gains, or just for protection against market risk over a particular time. You are assured of a certain price that meets your goals. Of course, your company's stock must allow for you to enter into a hedging contract.

What is a collar?

A collar involves buying a put and selling a call on your stock. This creates a floor and a cap for your stock price. The cost of the put can be off-set by the premium you receive from selling the call. A European option is exercisable only on a given date. By using European options for your put and call, you can protect the value of your options at the vesting date. However, you must be careful not to create a constructive sale when you design your collar. Otherwise you could be treated as having sold the stock (IRC Section 1259).

What is a straddle?

A straddle involves the purchase or sale of a put and call at the same exercise price with the same expiration date. If you wanted to protect yourself from a large move in your company's stock up or down, then you would use a straddle.

What is a synthetic short?

In a **synthetic short** you buy a put, sell a call, and buy a risk-free bond (T-bill). The math is complex, but the basic result is to protect the value of your equity position.

What is a variable pre-paid forward?

A variable pre-paid forward contract is an agreement with a brokerage firm that establishes a floor and a ceiling on the price of your stock at a future date (e.g.: the date of vesting). So long as the market price is within that range, you will receive the market price for your shares. If the price is above or below the ceiling and floor, the brokerage firm either realizes a profit or a loss. With a variable pre-paid forward contract, you lock-in the price (within a range), postpone taxes until the close of the contract, and get an advance on some of your sales proceeds.

This is a very brief review of a very complex topic. Be sure to seek expert advice before considering any hedging approaches.

If my stock is not publically traded can I still use these techniques?

You could use a publically traded stock that closely resembles your company's stock performance as a surrogate for your own stock.

If my options aren't vested, is there a way I can lock in a price?

Yes. If we are talking about a substantial value, then you may want to consider a collar. Let's say that your options are worth $1,000,000. You are confident about your company's potential, but don't want to assume the risk. You would buy a put option giving you the right to sell your stock at a specific price on a specific date. At the same time, you would sell a call option granting someone else the right to buy your shares at a specific price on a specific date. Puts and calls are discussed in Chapter One. The put and call are only exercisable as of a specific date, the date that you can exercise your stock options (a European option). If the price of your company's stock goes above the option price, the buyer of the call buys your shares away from you as of the date you exercise your stock options. If the share price goes below your price, you put the shares to the seller of the put. In either case, you have locked in a price that is acceptable to you. If the stock skyrockets, the increase belongs to the buyer of the call. If you've done a great job of estimating the stock price at the date of exercise, then both the put and call will expire unexercised, and you will keep the stock. If your options are ISOs and the stock is called or put, then you would have a disqualifying distribution.

How do I use Qualified Small Business stock to defer taxes?

If you are holding shares in a **Qualified Small Business** (QSB), and you have decided that you want to do something about your concentrated risk, then there may be some help. First, though, you need to know if you have QSB stock. Your stock may qualify if: you bought or received your shares directly from a corporation (e.g., through the exercise of an option); the corporation started up after mid 1993 and had gross assets of $50 million or less prior to and immediately after issuance of the stock; the corporation meets an "active business" test, and is not involved in certain types of business, such as banking, farming, hotels, and professional service (e.g., engineering or consulting).

How do I defer paying taxes on the sale of QSB stock?

Internal Revenue Code Section 1045 allows you to sell your QSB stock and defer paying on the gain if you rollover the proceeds into new QSB stock within 60 days from the date of sale. To qualify, you must meet a number of conditions.

Two of the more significant requirements are that you must have held your original QSB stock for more than six months and you must elect to apply the rollover provisions of Section 1045. You make the election on your income tax return for the tax year in which the original QSB stock is sold.

The deferral is available only to the extent that you would have had capital gains on the sale. If the sale involves a disqualifying disposition of ISO stock, the post-exercise appreciation cannot be deferred; any ordinary income would be recognized.

No limits exist on how much you can rollover or how many times you can elect rollover treatment. The replacement stock doesn't have to be stock of only one company, you can rollover the proceeds into a diversified portfolio of QSBs and still defer the gain.

You should keep in mind, however, that while the tax has been deferred, it has not been eliminated. The basis of your old shares is carried over into your new shares. Unless you hold the new shares until your death or gift them to a charity, a tax will be due should you sell your QSB shares and do not qualify for a further rollover.

What happens if I sell my QSB shares and don't rollover?

Congress, in an effort to spur investment in small businesses, enacted IRS Code Section 1202, which provided a 50% exclusion of the gain. For a taxpayer in the 28% tax bracket or above, the enactment of Section 1202 reduced the tax rate on sales of certain QSB stock to 14%. Qualifying for the 14% tax rate, however, is a bit more complicated than qualifying for rollover treatment of gains. Some of the requirements that must be met include:

1) You must have held the QSB stock that is being sold for more than five years. Although your basis may have been determined as a result of Section 1045 rollovers, the holding period generally does not include the time those pre-QSB shares were held.

2) For any one taxpayer, the maximum amount of eligible gain with respect to the stock of a single issuer that may be subject to the 50% exclusion is the greater of $10 million or 10 times the taxpayer basis in the stock of the issuing corporation.

Even though this all may have started with nonqualified stock options, the AMT can creep into it. A portion of the gain excluded from gross income is added back to the taxable income for the purpose of computing alternative minimum taxable income.

What happens if I sell my QSB shares at a loss?

If your QSB shares satisfy the requirements of Section 1244, up to $100,000 each year of otherwise capital loss may be treated as an ordinary loss. If, after applying the limitation, the ordinary loss exceeds your net income for the year, the excess is available to offset income from prior and future years.

Is there anything similar if my company stock is not a QSB?

Yes. If your company stock does not qualify as a QSB, you could get similar benefits by investing in specialized small business investment companies (SSBIC). In 1993, the Small

Business Investment Act authorized the SBA to grant SSBIC licenses to investment companies that facilitate ownership of businesses by disadvantaged taxpayers. Congress subsequently repealed this provision, but SSBIC licenses issued prior to September 30, 1996, were not revoked. There are about 60 active SSBICs.

You can defer gains on the sale of publicly traded securities, provided sales proceeds are reinvested in an SSBIC within 60 days after the sale. Only capital gains may be deferred. Currently, any gain in excess of the investment in the SSBIC must be recognized currently. The amount of gain that you can rollover in a tax year is limited to the lesser of: 1) $50,000 or 2) $500,000, reduced by gains previously excluded. Code Section 1044 applies.

What happens when I sell my SSBIC interest?

If you sell at a gain, you may qualify for the 50% exclusion discussed above for QSB stock. However, the exclusion only applies to appreciation of the SSBIC and not to your original stock. If you sell at a loss, you may treat the loss as ordinary income loss. There is no dollar limit, however, as is the case with QSBs.

While the deferral of taxes is an appealing feature of both QSBs and SSBICs, it is important to recognize that these are very high risk investments, with limited liquidity, and mixed results for performance. You may be better off paying your taxes and investing in a diversified portfolio of quality stocks.

Chapter Fourteen

What Do I Do With All of This Information?

The key to employee stock option planning is to maximize the wealth of the employee through proper planning. Basically, there are four decisions that one can make when exercising options:

Exercise as soon as possible and sell.
Exercise as soon as possible and hold.
Exercise as late as possible and sell.
Exercise as late as possible and hold.

The variations on these four approaches are infinite especially when you add in multiple grants, reload features, ISOs and NQSOs, etc. In our planning we start with the four basic approaches, then modify them to meet each client's unique situation.

Beyond the stock option analysis there are all the other factors addressed in this book: cash to meet personal needs; concentration of investment in the employer's stock; estate planning issues; market volatility of the stock; how to pay for the exercise, etc.. The typical executive's income is dependent on the employer, retirement is dependent on the employer's retirement plan, health and welfare benefits are dependent on the employer, and, now, through stock options, the majority of his/her wealth is dependent on the success of the employer's stock. This is a very risky position. Many experts suggest selling when you exercise your options to avoid becoming too heavily invested in your company's stock. However, if you assume your company's stock will continue to rise faster than the market, then any analysis will show that you will maximize your benefit by leveraging the company's loan for as long as possible. That is, exercise as late as possible and hold.

Unfortunately, the driving strategy in stock option exercise planning has been to maximize the profits and minimize the taxes. Most advisers, myself included, recommend a more balanced approach which is to exercise and sell some options to reduce exposure to the risk of having "all of your eggs in one basket." Prior to Enron, clients didn't always appreciate the merit of this advice. They wanted to know why they had to sell the company stock just before it doubled. On the other hand, when holding after exercise made sense and the stock then went down in value, they wanted to know why we didn't sell. They were confusing stock option planning with stock forecasting.

Stock forecasting is not done very well, even by the experts. It should not be the primary factor in making decisions involving the exercise of your stock options. Even if your company's stock has been climbing by 50% a year and you think it will continue, it is unwise to have all of your income, benefits, and wealth tied up in a single company.

Our firm takes the approach of **Core Capital**™ in the development of plans for our stock option clients.

What is the Core Capital™ concept?

Core Capital™ is the sum that it will take to meet your goals without having to work anymore. It requires the development of a financial plan to determine the present value of your future needs and goals. Let's say that you want to pay off your mortgage, send the kids to pricey colleges, and retire at 55 with $100,000 of inflation adjusted annual income. Without doing an analysis, let's say that this requires $3,000,000 invested at 8%. Then $3,000,000 is your Core Capital™. Let's also assume that you are receiving new options on a regular basis, and your currently vested options are worth $2,000,000. You would want to exercise and sell options until you had your Core Capital™ set aside and were no longer subject to **concentrated risk**.

What is concentrated risk and why does it matter?

Concentrated risk comes from having too much exposure in a single asset or single asset class. With stock options, the concentration is particularly acute because not only does the employee hold substantial amounts of the employer's stock either directly or through proxy (the stock options), but additionally, through salary and benefits, the employee's entire financial security is tied to a single entity. If the company gets into trouble, the employee could find himself without a paycheck, health insurance, and retirement benefits while holding stock options that are now worthless.

When you are excited about your job and proud of your company, it may be hard to believe that you should have your money anyplace else. However, even great companies aren't always great investments. The following is a list of *Fortune's* "*Most Admired*" companies in 1989 and 1999. **See Table 14.1.**

Table 14.1

Most Admired 1989	Annual ret. 90 -99	Most Admired 1999
1. Merck	11.1%	Wal-Mart
2. Rubbermaid	2.4%	Merck
3. 3M	0.06%	Herman Miller
4. Philip-Morris	(1.2%)	Shell Oil
5. Wal-Mart	(1.3%)	Exxon
6. Exxon	(2.9%)	PepsiCo
7. PepsiCo	(5.0%)	3M
8. Boeing	(8.5%)	Philip-Morris
9. Herman Miller	(8.6%)	Boeing
10. Shell Oil	(14.4%)	Rubbermaid

We see from the chart above that leaders don't always remain leaders, and frequently become losers. In fact, betting on a single stock can be a disaster. Consider some companies that were considered growth leaders in the early 80s. **See Table 14.2.**

Stanford C. Bernstein & Co., Inc., Investment Research and Management, conducted a study on the success of growth companies over time. The study covered the years from 1965 to 1999. Of all of the growth stocks in the study only 38% were still in the growth category 5 years later, 16% remained 10 years later, and only 4% made it 20 years. Bernstein found that technology companies fared worst. Of 34 technology companies in the study at the start of 1980, only one, Intel, remained at the end of 1999. Bernstein points out "Back in 1980, you'd have been hard-pressed

Table 14.2

Growth early 80's	Ret. 82-84	Ret. 85-99
Intergraph	337.8%	(83%)
Ames Dept. Stores	298.6%	(100%)
Circle K	205.2%	(100%)
Shoney's	197.5%	(82.5%)
Data General	118.6%	(45.1%)
Pan Am	68.2%	(100%)
Wang Labs.	57.6%	(92.2%)

to distinguish Intel's potential from that of the other 33." Yet 20 years later, 23 were no longer trading, and of the 11 remaining only Intel and two others had beaten the performance of the S&P 500.

The 2001/2002 Bear market provided a fresh reminder of just how dangerous it can be to have all of your money tied up in one stock as share prices plummeted. **See Table 14.3.**

Table 14.3

Company	Beg. 2000	End 2001	% Change
Cisco	107.30	18.11	-83
General Electric	44.67	40.08	-10
Home Depot	56.63	51.01	-10
Intel	25.00	19.22	-23
Johnson & Johnson	93.25	59.10	-37
Lucent	75.00	6.30	-92
Microsoft	116.75	66.25	-43
Qualcomm	176.13	50.50	-71
Wal-Mart	69.13	57.55	-17

Hopefully, the preceding discussion on concentrated risk will have convinced you of the merits of our Core Capital™ concept. However, if you need a bit more convincing, here are two recent real life stories.

Horror Story Number One:

An executive was terminating employment, so he exercised 14,000 options at $6.44 when the stock was selling at $114 in 1999. Had he sold the shares at that time, he would have had over a $1.5 million gain. Instead, he held on believing the stock would go higher. The technology sell off of 2000 hit and his shares dropped to $58. His value dropped to $812,000. Yet he had $481,869 in taxes on the exercise! **See Table 14.4.**

Table 14.4

Exercise and sell		Exercise and hold	
Exercise cost ($6.44 x 14,000)	$90,160	Exercise cost + tax (prior column)	$572,029
FMV ($114 x 14,000)	$1,599,000	Current value ($58 x 14,000)	$812,000
Spread (FMV - EC)	$1,505,840	Net: after cost	$239,971
Tax @32%	$481,869	Tax savings from loss	???
Balance to Exec.	$1,117,131	Loss of value	$877,160

Horror Story Number Two:

This one, from the *Wall Street Journal* (7/10/2000), is the story of Jeffrey Sieff, age 30. In less than 24 months, Mr. Sieff went from a penniless Stanford M.B.A. graduate, to being worth more than $1.2 million, to owing $86,000 in taxes that he couldn't pay and living in an apartment without furniture.

Mr. Sieff joined Scient Corporation in 1998 with a salary of about $100,000 and 10,000 to 20,000 NQSOs at $1.10/share. In April 1999, Scient had an IPO, and Mr. Sieff exercised his options. In July 1999, Mr. Sieff figured he had it made and left Scient giving up 3 years of unvested options. Scient was going up so fast that Mr. Sieff figured he was making $10,000 per day. On March 9, 2000, Scient hit $130/share. Mr. Sieff decided to hold off selling shares to avoid a short-term gain that would cost him an extra $100,000 in taxes. He figured he would ". . . still be ahead so long as his Scient's shares didn't fall below $100,000 in the next two weeks." "I was gambling," he says. "Wouldn't you wait two weeks for $100,000?"

Scient's shares dropped to the mid 60's. Mr. Sieff sold some shares and used the money for taxes and bought some other Internet stocks. By April 17, 2000, Scient's shares ($130/share just 5 weeks earlier) were at $30.25/share. Mr. Sieff's net worth had plummeted 78% and he still owed $86,000 in taxes.

The Wall Street Journal stated, "The free fall of many Internet stocks since April has forced thousands of Web Startups to abruptly scale down their lifestyle and expectations. While the lucky few at the top of the company ladder are still millionaires or even billionaires on paper, at least, a far larger number of Web-heads are living the tail end of the rags-to-riches-to-rags story. The pain is perhaps sharpest among the younger Net set, a generation that had never experienced a market downturn in their professional lives . . . some are giving up on buying homes or postponing having children."

Hopefully, we have made the point about concentrated risk. Prepare a financial plan and put your Core Capital™ aside first.

If you find yourself with underwater options, check Chapter Eight for guidance.

When should I exercise and sell?

The number one reason given for exercising and selling stock options is to buy a new boat, car, etc. This is a bad reason. There is the cost of exercising, the loss of future appreciation, etc. You must have a plan that considers your other resources, the volatility of your company's stock, and the stock market as a whole. What are your real needs for the money? What is your Core Capital™ requirement? Don't exercise too soon or wait too long.

An option is essentially an interest free loan from the company. There is no cost and no tax liability until you exercise. However, the price fluctuates and you may be forced to exercise at a bad time. You don't want to wait until the last minute!

One approach to avoid waiting till the last minute would be the **average out strategy.** You would begin a couple of years before the options' expiry date or your retirement and exercise some options regularly. This is a way of dollar cost averaging. While the price of the option may be the same, the spread and, therefore, the taxes and your basis will not be the same. The average out strategy may also be an effective way to control the impact of the AMT on the exercise of your ISOs.

Certainly you want to test the four methods mentioned at the beginning of this chapter to see what your tax consequences will be. However, you do not want to make a decision based on taxes alone. I believe that the Core Capital™ concept is far more important than projections based upon optimistic assumptions of how much more you will be worth by holding onto your options or company stock until the last minute.

While I have already discussed concentrated risk, an additional point is worth making. Some phenomenal successes have led us to believe that stock options are the way to instant wealth, but the reality is that more employees are disappointed by them than benefit from them. This has been especially true with startups. VentureOne, a venture capital research firm found that in 1987, only 22% of startup companies made it to an IPO. CommScan, an investment banking research firm, found that of 131 Internet IPOs in 1999, 58 were trading below their IPO price in 2000. The point is, make sure you get your Core Capital™ first!

Techniques to Defer Or Reduce Taxes on The Sale of Your Company's Stock

Are there ways to reduce the AMT tax on ISOs?

Exercise sooner rather than later. If you expect your company's stock to rise, then exercise when your options vest. AMT is based on the spread, the difference between the exercise price and the fair market value. The longer you wait to exercise, the greater the spread. By exercising early you will keep the spread down and reduce your AMT income.

Exercise as late as possible. If your company's stock has already appreciated substantially and an exercise would result in substantial AMT, don't exercise. Instead, use the funds you would have used to exercise your options to buy other stock instead. No exercise means no AMT. If you hold the other stock for 12 months you will pay only the 20% long-term capital gains tax. You can use the proceeds from the sale of the other stock to pay for the exercise of your ISO. **See Example 14.1.**

> ***Example 14.1*** You can spend $20,000 to exercise your ISOs or buy a portfolio of other stocks. Assume both your company's stock and the portfolio will each appreciate 25% over the next three years. If you exercise the option, you have AMT in the year of exercise of $500. You hold for the three years and sell the stock. You pay 20% long-term capital gains on $7500 leaving you with $6,000. <u>Your net from exercising the option $5,500</u>. Instead, you buy the portfolio for $20,000. You hold for three years and sell for $25,000 ($20,000 @25%). Your tax on the $5,000 gain is $1,000. You net $4,000. You then use your $20,000 to exercise your option. You sell immediately (a disqualifying distribution) resulting in ordinary taxes (no AMT) on the exercise. Your gain of $7,500 is taxed at ordinary rates (assume 31%) netting you $5,175. <u>Add the gain from the portfolio and you have $9,175.</u> Which would you rather have?

Make a disqualifying disposition in the year you exercise. If after getting some expert advice, you find that you would be better off paying ordinary income tax, sell your shares within the same tax year of exercise and disqualify the ISO. One planning technique is to exercise your ISOs early in the year. This gives you the rest of the year to decide whether to treat the exercise as an ISO or to disqualify it.

Chapter Fifteen

Where Can I Find More Information?

While I hope that you will find most of your questions answered in this book, the following references may be of additional value to you. After reading *An Executive's Guide*, the best source for more information is your professional advisor.

Books:

Consider Your Options
Author: Kaye Thomas

Granting Stock Options: An Approach to Designing Long-term Incentive for Employees
Author: George Paulin

Incentive Compensation and Employee Ownership
Author: Scott Rodrick

Stock Options: An Authoritative Guide to Incentive and Nonqualified Stock Options
>Author: Robert Pastore

Strictly Business
>Esperti Peterson Institute
>Contributing Author: Peter R. Wheeler, CLU, CHFC, CFP, CIMC

Sudden Money
>Author: Susan Bradley

The Seven Stages of Money Maturity
>Author: George Kinder

The Stock Options Book
>Author: David Johanson

Websites:

www.the-ef.org - Entrepreneurs Foundation

www.myStockOptions.com

www.sevenstages.com - from the *Seven Stages of Money Maturity*

www.smartmoney.com - Tax Guide

www.StockOptionsCentral.com

www.StockOptionServices.com

www.suddenmoney.com - from the *Sudden Money* book

www.wheelerfrost.com - this is the author's web site. Updates to this book will be provided through the web site as necessary, and links to other useful stock option web sites.